C0-APF-942

youth ice hockey

Consultants (AHAUS)

Hal Trumble, Executive Director
Ken Johannson, Chief Instructor
Gail Anderson (Editorial)

Consultants (Medical)

Gerard A. Engh, M.D.
Joseph M. Jares, M.D.

Contributors

Dave Peterson (Goaltending)
Pieter Kollen (Skating)
Rochester (Minn.) Youth Hockey Association

**Library of Congress
Catalog Card Number 79-109498**

**"Sports Techniques" Series
SBN 87670-072-5**

ⓒ *The Athletic Institute 1976*
All Rights Reserved

*Published by The Athletic Institute
Chicago, Illinois 60654*

Foreword

The importance of youth league programs cannot be overemphasized in their contribution to the enjoyment of young people and to their physical and character development. The purpose of The Athletic Institute is to support and encourage competitive athletics, and we have attempted to do this in many different ways. We hope that our series of sports manuals for coaches and players on youth league teams will contribute to high-quality performance and encourage participation in these very worthwhile programs.

The Athletic Institute is especially grateful to Ken Johannson of the Amateur Hockey Association of the United States, for his outstanding contributions in ice hockey techniques. Appreciation is also extended to Dave Peterson and Pieter Kollen for their fine demonstration of hockey fundamentals.

D. E. Bushore
Executive Director
The Athletic Institute

Table of Contents

Introduction

Throughout the United States, more than a million youngsters participate in youth ice hockey sponsored by private, public, civic and church organizations.

It is our purpose in this publication to give you, the youth league player, the techniques to help you become a better player.

Your coach will spend many hours on the field teaching you the skills to play the great game of hockey. What will help you, your coach and eventually the team in the long run is the time you spend after practice time studying the basic moves of your position.

We hope the diagrams, photos and description of hockey fundamentals provided on the following pages will help you become the player you desire to be.

Fred C. Engh
National Consultant
Youth Programs
The Athletic Institute

the youth league ice hockey player

So you've finally made it. After watching all those pro games and dreaming of the day you'd be playing ice hockey yourself, you're finally there. You're about to get your own uniform and follow in the footsteps of Bobby Orr, Gordy Hull and all your favorite players.

But what about playing ice hockey? Sure, it's going to be great fun, but did you ever stop to think why your Mom and Dad let you join the program and why your coach will spend many hours teaching you how to play the game?

Right now it may be hard to understand, but aside from all the fun you will have playing ice hockey, the adults responsible for letting you play feel certain that not only will you be getting a lot of great exercise, having a lot of fun and naturally learning a lot about what it takes to be a good ice hockey player, but also you'll be developing into a better person.

For example, when your Dad has a rough day at his job it's much like losing a game. If you learn through playing ice hockey that after losing a game you've got to keep trying and not give up, then maybe it will help you through many "losing" days in your life. Or how about when things cause adults to lose their cool. They realize that getting mad and upset won't help them in the long run, just as you will learn in ice hockey that when things don't go your way, getting angry just makes everything worse. When you're mad, you're less able to be calm and be yourself, and therefore to be at your best.

Aside from these things, playing ice hockey gives you a chance to make new friends and helps you understand that to be successful as a team, you have to cooperate with your teammates and be loyal to them even when you want to give up. Many situations you will encounter in playing ice hockey will teach you about life and how to get along with others.

So look forward to many fine hours ahead playing ice hockey. Play it well, and you will be rewarded in many different ways.

Responsibility of the Player to the Coach

Your coach is a person who gives many hours of his time just for you, hoping you will learn many of the things which will help you become a good ice hockey player. In ice hockey, the name of the game is learning to do your best because many times the difference between doing well and doing your best means a loss or a win for your team. Therefore, at all times it is your responsibility to give your coach your very best effort. That means paying close attention to his instructions and obeying the rules he has set up.

In ice hockey there are many things to learn. For instance, every play the coach designs includes a special assignment for you. It may be learning to make a pass at the right time, understanding how to change direction "on a dime" or just being in the proper position at all times. In any case, your coach has designed a play which he feels will score a goal for your team. It will be your responsibility to know your job and be ready to perform at the right instant. The end result might spell success for your team.

To the Referee

Every competitive game has to have someone to enforce the rules and the purpose of rules is to make playing the game fair for all.

A referee does not have an easy job because he must constantly make accurate decisions on the play of the game. The ice hockey referee wants to do as good a job as he can to make the game fair for both teams and he needs your help to do his job. Therefore, ice hockey players have the responsibility of listening and cooperating with the referees of the game at all times. Most important, since he has the authority to make these decisions, the referee has the right to the respect, not the abuse, of players, coach and spectators.

The following code of behavior might help to make youth ice hockey the experience it should be.

ICE
H—**Have** patience with the referee.
O—**Objecting** to a decision made by the officials is not the right of a player.
C—Your **coach** may discuss decisions with the referee—don't interfere.
K—**Keep** your emotions under control.
E—Don't **embarrass** your coach by abusing the referee.
Y—**Your** attitude toward officials can affect your enjoyment of the game.

To Yourself

Playing ice hockey means you must make certain sacrifices. It means you must attend practices called by your coach. You must eat properly and get enough hours of sleep, learn your assignments as best you can on all plays and work hard at all that goes with being a winning ice hockey player.

As a member of your family, you should let your parents know well in advance of when practices and games are scheduled, especially if you need transportation. Also, it would be a nice gesture to invite your parents, brothers and sisters to the games. Your invitation shows your interest in them and they in turn will respond to you.

To Yourself (continued)

Above all else, playing youth ice hockey should be fun. Sure, things will be tough at times—such as missing an easy shot, icing or causing an unnecessary penalty—but it's all part of playing ice hockey. If you do make a mistake (as even the pros do), be sure it wasn't because you weren't prepared or, worst of all, didn't try. Then and only then will playing youth ice hockey be the enjoyable time you thought it would be.

equipment

What Equipment, and of What Quality, Is Necessary at Various Skill Levels?

The **minimum** at any level are skates, stick, helmet, mouthguard and jersey.

Of increasing importance at higher age and skill levels (in order of need) are elbow pads, shin guards, gloves, hockey pants and shoulder pads.

All boys should wear a protective cup and supporter by age ten, or earlier if playing in very competitive leagues. Once players start wearing hockey pants, hockey stockings also are necessary.

Players should wear **all** of their hockey equipment **all** of the time they are on the ice. By the time a boy has advanced beyond the novice level, he should wear all of the above-mentioned protective equipment.

A few words about **quality** are in order. As a general rule, the better-quality equipment is the best buy in the long run. While it is possible to be extravagant and pay too much for equipment, the more common practice is paying too little.

Skates

Skates are the most important part of a player's equipment. Buy good quality. This frequently means buying the more expensive, particularly as players enter the experienced level of competition. For beginners, medium-priced skates usually are acceptable. In most communities, sporting goods stores operate skate exchanges which frequently are a source of good used skates.

Above all, make sure they fit now. Be sure the heel of the foot doesn't move around in the boot. There should be some room for growth (about one-half to one inch is plenty); an extra pair of sox can help "fill up" the boot, but wearing more than two pair indicates that the skates are too big.

The leather on the ankle of the boot should have body and firmness. **Caution:** When this part of the skate becomes flimsy, the skate usually is done for.

Lacing of skates is important. All players must learn as early as possible to lace their own skates. Generally it is best to lace them up "snug," but not so tight as to cut off circulation in the foot.

The **lower eyelets** are the least important, but lacing in this area should be tight enough to pull the leather up against the side of the foot. The **middle eyelets** are most important, and it is possible to lace too tightly in this area; pull laces "comfortably snug." For the **top two or three eyelets,** laces can be pulled somewhat tighter than in the middle section. Again, avoid lacing too tightly and thus constricting circulation in the foot. Be sure to lace to the top.

The lace should be tied in a bow at the front of the boot. Wrapping extra lace around the ankle does no good and may be a hindrance if the laces slip up onto the shin and in the process become too loose. Solution: Use shorter laces.

Rubbing on the ankle under the knot, commonly called "lace bite," can be avoided by placing a small (2" x 3" x ½") piece of foam rubber between the tongue of the boot and the ankle.

How often to **sharpen** skate blades is a personal thing, but for most effective skating the edges of the blades should have a feel of sharpness to them. This usually means sharpening every two to three weeks, more often on outdoor ice.

Helmets

The one-piece helmet provides the most strength, but the two-piece helmet provides adequate strength and the advantage of adjustable size for comfort and for accommodating growth. Best advice: Buy a good helmet, but not necessarily the most expensive.

Mouthguards

The relative merits of inside versus outside mouthguards is unsettled; wearing both settles the dispute. Whichever type, make sure you wear mouthguards in the proper position at all times.

Elbow Pads

These are very important for all players, including beginners because of the number of times they fall. Elbow pads are not expensive, but they will prevent many an injury.

Gloves

A little extra money for gloves usually is a good investment, although in recent years tougher protective material has been added to some of the less-expensive gloves.

Clothing

Players should dress appropriately for the conditions. For outside hockey, a light jacket or sweatshirt under the hockey jersey is a good idea. With other protective equipment, use common sense. Hockey pants provide fibre or shock-absorbing protection for the hips and "tail bone," and shin pads provide the same for the lower legs.

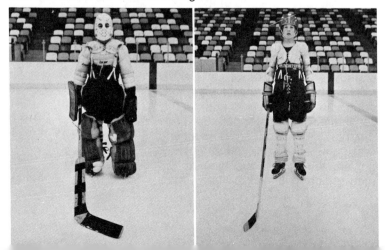

Sticks

Hockey sticks are made in "left," "right" and "neutral" models. Generally, a left-hand shooter (shoots from the left side of his body) should use a "left" model; a right-hand shooter, a "right" model. However, the "neutral" model is recommended for beginning players. Curved or "hooked" blades should not be used until the player has learned stick-handling and shooting fundamentals.

Selecting the Correct Lie and Length

The **lie** of a stick refers to the angle between the blade and the shaft: the smaller the angle, the higher the lie. A guide to proper lie: In normal skating position with stick on the ice in front of the body, most of the blade should be flat on the ice. Most boys will use lie #5 or #6. A low lie (#3 or #4) puts the blade, and therefore the puck, farthest from the feet. A high lie (#7) brings the blade and the puck closer to the player's feet.

HIGH LIE
6 OR 7

LOW LIE
3 OR 4

To determine the proper **length** of the stick, place the end of the blade on the ice between your skates, with the shaft straight up in front of your body. Proper length is between the chin and the tip of the nose, or slightly shorter. Cut off the extra length of shaft. If you have trouble controlling the stick and puck at the recommended length, cut off an additional one to two inches. As a general rule, sticks of young hockey players tend to be too long rather than too short.

14

Taping

Taping saves wear on the blade and provides a better surface for controlling the puck. The question of taping from heel to toe or from toe to heel has been debated by hockey people for years. Heel to toe seems better, for the overlap of the tape provides resistance to help keep the puck from sliding off the blade.

1. **SECURE TAPE WITH OVERLAP WRAP.**
2. **SUBSEQUENT TAPING OVERLAPS PREVIOUS WRAP BY ONE-HALF.**
3. **PULL TAPE FIRMLY.**

A knob or bulge of tape at the end of the shaft helps keep the stick from sliding out of the player's hands.

1. **FIRST TWO OR THREE LAPS ONE ON TOP OF OTHER.**
2. **CONTINUE TAPING UNTIL DESIRED SIZE KNOB IS ATTAINED.**

Proper-Fitting Equipment

1. **Helmet** . . . *should be sized at the time of purchase or adjusted to fit properly. The front edge of the helmet should extend ½ inch to ¾ inch beyond the forehead. The chin strap should be fastened.*

2. **Shoulder Pads** . . . *should be adjusted to fit the player. Fiber cap should extend to the tip of the shoulder.*

3. **Elbow Pads** . . . *should be held snugly in place, with the fiber cap over the point of the elbow.*

4. **Pants** . . . *should be held in proper position by suspenders. Pads protect the lower spine, hips and thighs.*

5. **Shin pads** . . . *should be of proper length to protect knee and shin, and should be held in place by tape or elastic straps over the stockings.*

6. **Skates** . . . *should fit now, with no more than ½ inch for growth.*

III-Fitting Equipment

1. **Helmet** . . . *loose fit with chin strap hanging loose.*

2. **Shoulder Pads** . . . *fiber caps extending too far beyond the tip of the shoulder. Protective extensions cut off to save weight.*

3. **Elbow Pads** . . . *no fiber caps.*

4. **Pants** . . . *too big and hanging too low. Protective pads are not in the proper position to prevent injury.*

5. **Shin Pads** . . . *too long or not held in place by tape or straps.*

6. **Skates** . . . *bought to "be good for two years"; result: too big this year, too small the next.*

skating

The Skate Blade

Hockey is a fast-moving, hard-hitting sport. None of its excit-
ing action can take place, however, without two often-neg-
lected factors — the ice and the skate blade. The following
focuses on why a blade glides (moves smoothly over the ice)
and how to improve the performance of the skater from the
beginner to the advanced "power skater."

A speed skate has a longer blade than a hockey skate: the
more blade against the ice, the faster and longer the glide. If a
blade were flat from toe to heel, however, you would glide in
a straight line and never turn, so blades have a radius (or
rocker) which facilitates turns. Most good blades come cor-
rectly designed so that the flat part of the blade in the middle
gives maximum glide and the rockered sections at the front
and back enable the skater to make quick turns.

The Grind

Blades should have a "hollow" grind (see illustration). A deep
hollow should be used on very cold ice surfaces. The disad-
vantage of a deep grind is that it is brittle and the fine edges of
the blade are lost more quickly than on those not sharpened
as deeply. A shallow grind lasts longer, but does not grip or
cut into the ice as well as a deep grind. For either grind —
deep or shallow — it is of utmost importance that the skate
and the grinding stone be level.

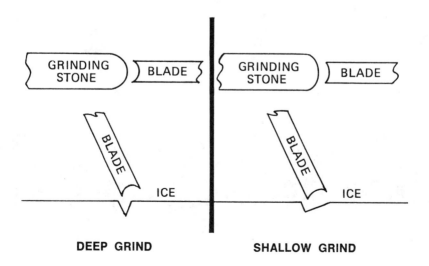

DEEP GRIND   **SHALLOW GRIND**

Skating Forward

Fundamental to the success of any hockey player is his ability to skate well.

Skating is "gliding"; the blade glides because when it is pushed against the ice it creates friction. Friction creates heat and the blade melts the ice. The greater the weight pushed against the ice, the longer the glide — that is to say "controlled weight," which is weight that creates the least amount of disturbance between the blade and the ice.

When gliding forward, weight should be toward the back of the blade, but not on the heels. Bend the knees and drive forward with the trailing leg. Keep skates close to the ice and push off with power, alternating with one skate and then the other. A smooth skating movement flows from the hips with long, gliding leg strokes.

1. **CROUCH FORWARD WITH WEIGHT PRESSING TOWARD MIDDLE/BACK AREA OF SKATE BLADE.**

2. **KNEES ARE BENT.**

3. **WEIGHT ON PUSHING (POWER) FOOT.**

4. **PUSH (EXPAND) AGAINST ICE TO SIDE (NOT BACK).**

5. **KNEE OF GLIDING LEG STAYS BENT, KEEPING BODY DOWN.**

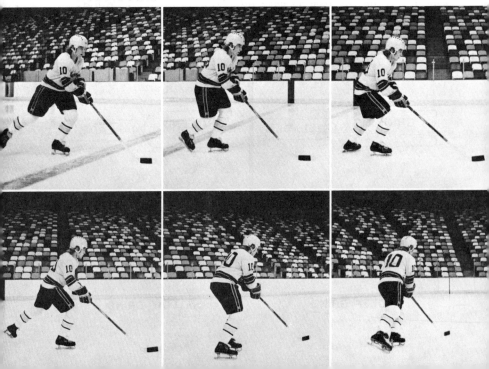

6. EXPAND POWER LEG AND FOOT COMPLETELY,
   THEN RETURN TO BASIC POSITION.

7. SMOOTH SKATING MOVEMENT FLOWS FROM
   HIPS WITH LONG GLIDING LEG STROKES.

Skating Backward

Skate in a crouched (sitting) position with knees bent and buttocks low to the ice. When skating backward, weight should be back of the ball of the foot.

Leg and foot action should be very much like forward skating — pushing hard to the side against the ice.

1. SKATE FROM SITTING POSITION.
2. BEND KNEE OF GLIDING LEG.
3. PUSH TO SIDE WITH WHOLE BLADE.
4. COMPLETELY EXPAND POWER LEG AND FOOT AGAINST ICE.
5. RETURN POWER LEG TO BASIC POSITION SO IT CAN BECOME GLIDING LEG ON NEXT STROKE.

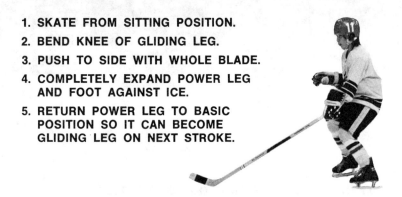

6. TOP HAND ON STICK. USE OTHER HAND FOR BALANCE.

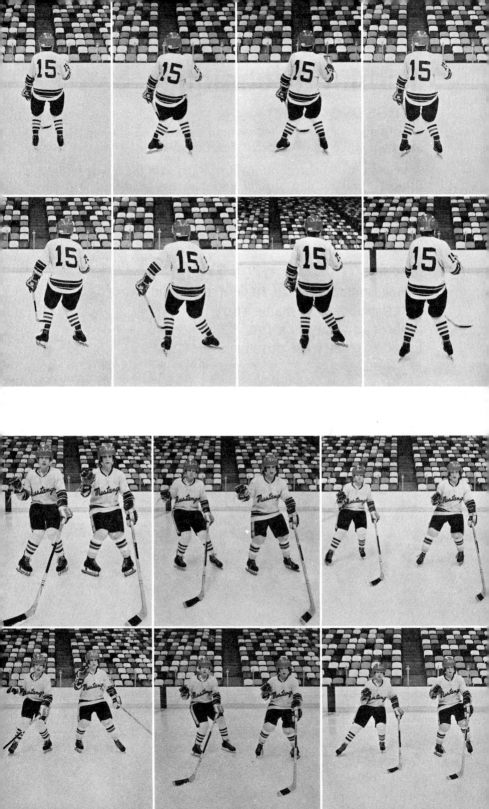

Turning Techniques

Crossover Turn

This turn is made to the left or right by crossing one leg over the other while skating forward or backward.

With knees well bent, control your weight over the inside foot. Bring the outside leg around and over the inside leg while leaning toward the direction of the turn.

Maintain good body control and push off the outside leg. Keep inside shoulder up and inside body line firm.

Forward Crossover Turn

1. PUSH INSIDE HIP INTO TURN, KEEP INSIDE SHOULDER UP.
2. KEEP WEIGHT ON INSIDE FOOT.
3. DRIVE WITH OUTSIDE LEG.
4. CROSS OVER WITH OUTSIDE LEG.

Back Crossover Turn

This maneuver might better be described as "pull-togethers."
It is important that the upper body be kept firm and that the
inside shoulder is up and back. You "lead" with this shoulder.

1. REACH INTO CIRCLE WITH INSIDE FOOT.
2. PLACE WEIGHT ON BOTH FEET.
3. PULL ON INSIDE EDGE OF INSIDE LEG,
   PULLING BOTH FEET TOGETHER.
4. CROSS OUTSIDE LEG OVER IN FRONT OF INSIDE LEG.
5. PLACE WEIGHT ON OUTSIDE LEG.
6. REPEAT NUMBER 1 ABOVE.

Glide Turn

The glide turn is strong and quick and can be especially effective for carrying the puck around a defensive player.

Start by gliding forward in a straight line with weight toward the back of the blades and knees bent. If making a turn to the left, the left foot will move forward of the right foot about one to one and one-half feet. Use the outside edge of the left foot and the inside edge of the right foot to make the glide turn to the left.

The natural lean of the body is into the circle, but if you want to make a quick, sharp turn, lean the upper part of the body out of the circle. This helps push the heels around in a tighter rotation or circle.

For turning to the right, the same techniques are used except that the right foot leads, using the outside edge, while the left foot glides on the inside edge.

1. **BOTH FEET ON ICE, KNEES BENT FOR SOLID BASE.**
2. **EXTEND HIP NEAREST OPPONENT TOWARD DEFENSIVE PLAYER (TO INSIDE OF TURN).**
3. **HANDS EXTEND TO OPPOSITE SIDE.**
4. **KNEE OF INSIDE LEG WELL BENT. PUSH HARD AGAINST ICE WITH INSIDE EDGE OF SKATE ON OUTSIDE LEG (LIKE SKATING STROKE, BUT KEEP SKATE ON ICE).**
5. **INSIDE SHOULDER UP.**

Front-to-Back and Back-to-Front Turns

Changing directions quickly is an integral part of almost all hockey play. A team on offense suddenly becomes the team on defense and all players must react instantly.

Applying quick turn techniques properly permits the players to make these position adjustments as the situation merits while maintaining momentum in the same direction.

Back-to-Front Turn

1. PLACE WEIGHT ON NON-TURNING SIDE.
2. WITH HEELS TOGETHER, OPEN FEET AND BODY TO BEGIN TURN.
3. SHIFT WEIGHT FROM GLIDING LEG TO OPPOSITE FOOT.
4. COMPLETE TURN AND DRIVE OFF TRAILING LEG.

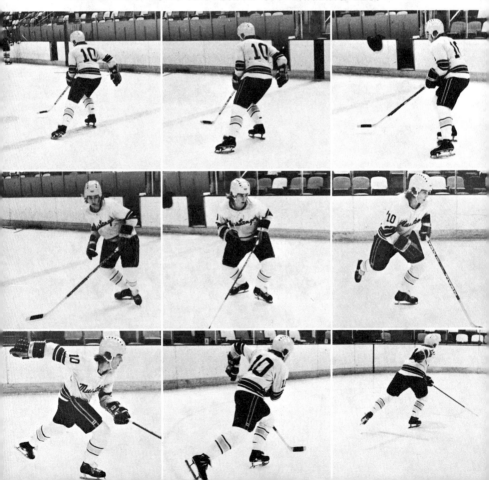

Front-to-Back Turn

1. SKATE FORWARD. AS WEIGHT IS TRANSFERRING TO GLIDING (FRONT) LEG . . .
2. ROTATE BODY TO DESIRED SIDE.
3. PUSH OFF POWER (BACK) LEG WITH SLIGHT JUMP, ENOUGH TO CLEAR ICE.
4. COMPLETE ROTATION OF BODY.
5. TURN FRONT FOOT 180 DEGREES AND LAND ON FOOT, SHIFTING WEIGHT TO THIS FOOT.
6. ASSUME BASIC POSITION FOR BACK STRAIGHT-LINE SKATING.

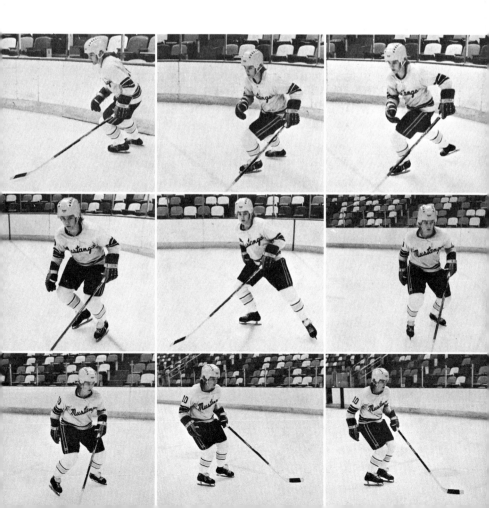

Stopping

Stopping can be accomplished in three ways: stopping with both feet, stopping on the front foot and stopping on the back foot.

Stopping with both feet is usually the easiest and surest stop to make. Stopping on the back foot is often best in preparation for a backcheck, while stopping on the front foot permits a quick direction change.

Stopping with Both Feet

Keep weight evenly distributed on both feet and turn feet perpendicular to the skating line, causing the blades to "skid" against the ice.

1. DISTRIBUTE WEIGHT EVENLY ON BOTH FEET.
2. LEAN SLIGHTLY BACK FROM POINT OF STOP, BUT TRY TO KEEP WEIGHT OVER FEET.
3. STOP WITH BOTH FEET, THEN PROCEED AS DESIRED.

Back Stop with Both Feet

Players may wish to stop while skating backward by turning the heels of both feet "in" and leaning forward, keeping the knees well bent. This is the most "sudden" backward stop.

Many players find it easier to backstop on one foot. To make this stop, turn the heel of the gliding foot inward while keeping the knees bent to cushion the abruptness of the stop.

1. **WHILE GLIDING BACKWARD, TURN HEEL OF GLIDING FOOT INWARD.**

2. **BEND KNEES AS WHEN MAKING ALL STOPS.**

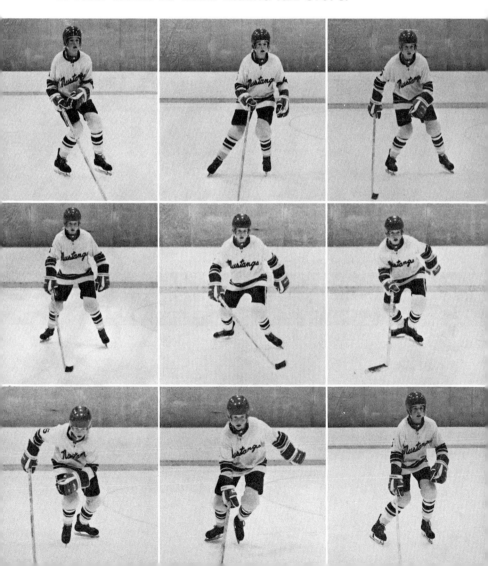

Stopping with Back Foot

Stopping on the back foot is probably the most difficult way to stop since so much pressure is brought to bear on the entire leg from hip to foot.

To make this stop, lean away from the stopping point. Weight is shifted entirely to the back leg with the front foot off the ice.

At the completion of the stop, plant the free foot back on the ice (usually with crossover stride) and proceed in the desired direction.

1. LEAN AWAY FROM STOP.
2. TRANSFER WEIGHT ENTIRELY OVER BACK LEG WHILE FORWARD FOOT COMES OFF ICE.
3. STOP ON BACK FOOT.
4. COMPLETE STOP. PLANT FREE FOOT ON ICE.
5. PROCEED IN DESIRED DIRECTION.

Stopping on Front Foot

This stop makes quick lateral movements possible.

Weight is shifted to forward leg and foot as back foot comes off the ice. As with other stopping methods, lean away from the stopping point. Stop on the front foot.

Re-position the back foot upon the ice and push off in another direction.

1. **SHIFT WEIGHT OVER FRONT LEG. BACK FOOT COMES OFF ICE.**

2. **LEAN AWAY FROM STOPPING POINT.**

3. **WITH STOP COMPLETED, RE-PLANT BACK SKATE ON ICE AND PUSH OFF IN ANOTHER DIRECTION.**

stickhandling

Next to skating, stickhandling is the most important hockey fundamental. Until the player, especially the novice, learns to control the puck, his ability to shoot and pass is severely limited. There are many more situations in a game that involve stickhandling than shooting.

The purpose of stickhandling, it should be emphasized, is to "fool" the defensive player. Otherwise, pushing the puck is the fastest means of travel.

Holding the Stick

Good stickhandling begins with the proper lie. The length of the stick also is important (see Equipment section). Whether a player becomes a left-hand or right-hand shot should depend on what is comfortable for him. There is nothing wrong with young players trying both ways, but once a decision has been made, switching should be avoided.

Hand Position

The top hand should be at the top of the shaft. There should be a gap of about one fist (six to eight inches with gloves on) between the top and bottom hands. The reason for this "high" position of the hands is to provide the widest possible reach while retaining control of the puck; the lower the bottom hand is on the shaft, the less side-to-side stickhandling movement the player has.

Hold the stick in front of the body, with arms free from the body. Hold the stick firmly, but not tightly. Slide the hands across the body to the fullest extent to each side when stickhandling, moving them together as one unit. Cup the blade of the stick over the puck.

Stickhandling Techniques

The basic "dribbles" are: **side-to-side** in front of the body, **front-to-back** at the side of the body and **diagonal** (beside the body on one side to forward of the body on the opposite side). Once the player has mastered these basic moves, combinations of the three can provide an unlimited variety of additional moves.

Novice players should first learn to push the puck, then learn to stickhandle side-to-side. They may have trouble with the front-to-back and diagonal moves, but intermediate players should be able to learn them, and experienced players master them.

A hockey player should learn to use a form of split vision. By aiming his center of vision about 30 to 40 feet in front of him, he should be able to see the puck, where he is going, where teammates are and, most important, where the opposition is.

Dribble Techniques

The *side-to-side* or *lateral dribble* is the most commonly used dribble in hockey.

The puck is controlled from side to side in a path which may vary in width from a few inches to as far as you can reach with the stick.

Proper hand position is extremely important. Placing hands too far apart limits lateral reach and control.

1. **TOP PHOTOS SHOW PROPER HAND POSITION AND RESULTING LATERAL REACH.**

2. **BOTTOM PHOTOS SHOW IMPROPER HAND PLACEMENT (HANDS TOO FAR APART) AND RESULTING LIMIT OF LATERAL REACH.**

Begin with the side-to-side move in front of the body, first standing still and then moving. Be sure to move the stick and hands completely across the body to the fullest extension of reach on both sides.

1. BASIC SKATING POSITION.

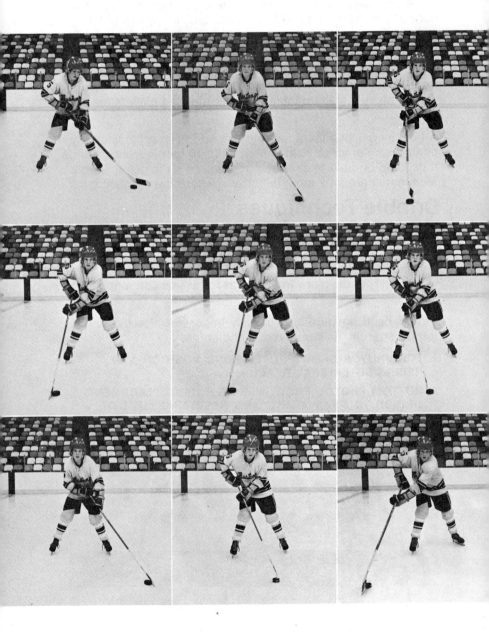

2. FOCUS EYES 30 TO 40 FEET AHEAD AND
   USE SPLIT VISION.
3. TO CONTROL THE PUCK, CUP THE STICK BLADE.
4. CONTROL THE PUCK IN FRONT WHILE MOVING THE
   PUCK FROM SIDE TO SIDE.

The *front-to-back dribble* is more difficult to execute, therefore requiring more practice. This dribble is often employed in play around an opponent's net or used to tempt an opposing player to go for the puck. Particularly good while skating toward a defensive player who is moving toward you; also very helpful in setting up a fake shot with a defenseman screening in front of the net.

1. BASIC SKATING POSITION. KEEP HEAD UP. WATCH PUCK WITH SPLIT VISION.

2. CUP THE STICK TO CONTROL PUCK.

3. FROM THE SIDE, CONTROL PUCK BACK TO FRONT AND THEN BACK.

4. PRACTICE WHILE STANDING STILL AND THEN WHILE MOVING.

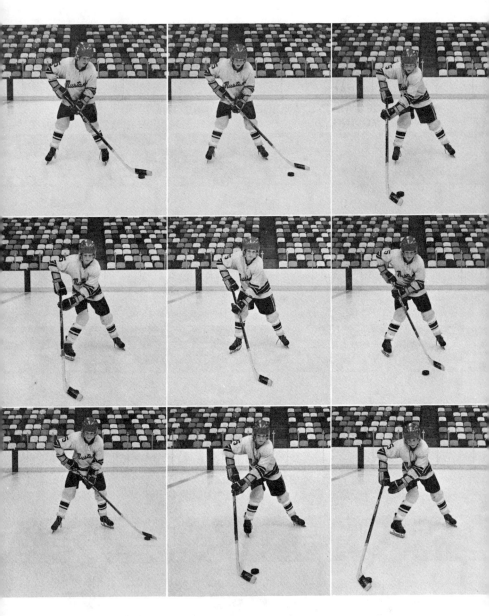

1. FOR DIAGONAL MOVE PLACE PUCK AT SIDE OF
   BODY AS IF TO SHOOT FOREHAND SHOT.
2. BRING PUCK FORWARD, THEN ACROSS BODY WITH A
   SHARP DIAGONAL MOVE TO OPPOSITE SIDE.
3. REACH AS FAR FORWARD AS POSSIBLE.
   CUP PUCK WITH BLADE.

The *diagonal dribble* is especially effective when combined with other moves such as pushing the puck between the stick and the body of an opposing player. Place the puck at the side of the body as if about to shoot a forehand shot, then bring the puck across diagonally to the opposite side of the body as far forward as you can reach.

passing and receiving

While skating and stickhandling are the most important hockey skills, a considerable amount of time should be devoted to the fundamentals of passing. Generally, the team that "moves" the puck well is the team that wins.

Passing moves the puck faster than stickhandling. To prove this point, try to "race" the passed puck; the puck always wins.

Hand Position

Move the lower hand four to six inches down the shaft from the stickhandling position; this should put about 8 to 14 inches between the hands. As a young player becomes stronger, he may want to bring his lower hand up the shaft toward the stickhandling position.

1. MOVE LOWER HAND FOUR TO SIX INCHES DOWN SHAFT FROM STICKHANDLING POSITION.

2. HANDS ARE THEN 8 TO 14 INCHES APART.

Passing Techniques

Push (or sweep) the pass to the target. Don't "slap" the puck. Push the puck and follow through, with the blade of the stick on or near the ice surface. The pass can be made by moving both hands toward the target, or by a push-pull action with the lower hand moving toward the target and the upper hand away. It is imperative that players learn to pass equally well forehand and backhand from in front of the body with the puck on the skating line. As beginners, most players will pass to the backhand side by moving the puck to the side of the body and passing forehand.

The pass should be hard enough to "go through" (beyond) the target, but soft enough to enable the receiver to control it. The pass that falls short of the target is perhaps the worst pass in hockey.

Aiming is the hard part of passing, but usually it is not too difficult when players are standing still. It still is not too difficult when only one player is moving, but there are all kinds of problems when both the passer and intended receiver are moving. Remember, the pass must lead the moving target. Once a player really understands the concept of leading the receiver, how much to lead becomes only a matter of judgment and experience.

1. LOOK AT TARGET.
2. SWEEP PUCK, MOVING BOTH HANDS TOWARD TARGET.
3. FOLLOW THROUGH KEEPING BLADE LOW TO ICE SURFACE.
4. APPLY SAME TECHNIQUES WHEN MAKING BACKHAND PASS.

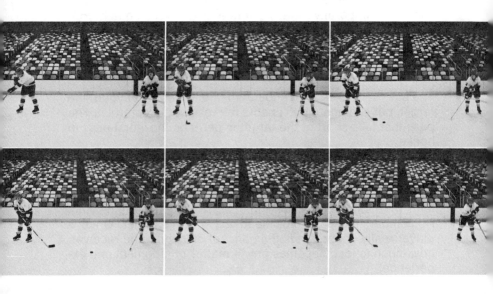

Back Pass

A back pass is particularly useful in making a return pass to a teammate in the offensive zone.

Before making the pass, make absolutely sure your teammate is open. If intercepted, this pass could give an opponent a great opportunity.

1. **TURN TO MAKE SURE TEAMMATE IS OPEN. DON'T PASS BLINDLY.**

2. **APPLY ALL BASIC PASSING TECHNIQUES.**

Flip Pass Techniques

This type of pass is used to clear the puck over an opponent's stick.

To lift the puck off the ice, first position the puck at the toe of the stick blade.

With a flicking motion of the wrists, flip the puck over your opponent's stick and to a teammate.

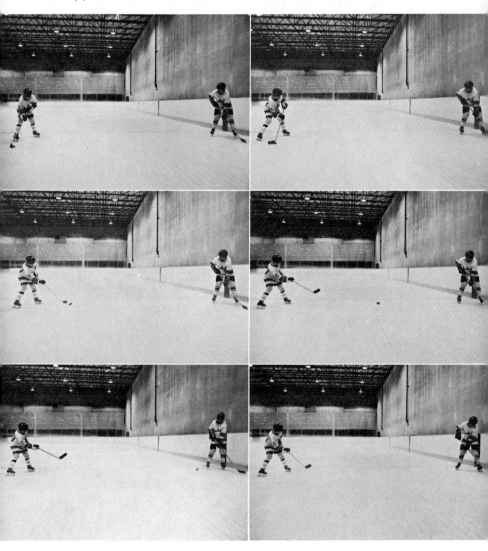

1. POSITION PUCK AT TOE OF STICK.
2. FLICK WRISTS TO LIFT PUCK.
3. BE READY FOR RETURN PASS.
4. SAME TECHNIQUES APPLY WHEN MAKING BACKHAND FLIP PASS.

Drop Pass Techniques

In making a *drop pass,* be absolutely certain to stop the puck completely. Do not permit the puck to continue to move. This will help a teammate from over-skating the puck.

To stop the puck, make a forward dribble, then cup the stick over the puck to keep it from moving.

Primarily, a drop pass is used in the offensive game inside the blue line.

1. CUP STICK OVER PUCK.
2. STOP PUCK COMPLETELY.
3. TEAMMATE PICKS UP PUCK.

Receiving the Pass

1. KEEP BLADE ON ICE TO PROVIDE GOOD TARGET.
2. MAINTAIN BASIC SKATING POSITION.

Three words summarize the important concepts in receiving a pass — give, cup and right angle.

To receive a pass, the receiver must get the blade of the stick out toward the pass (on the pass line) and move the blade in the same direction as the pass, only more slowly so as to allow the puck to gently come in contact with his stick blade. This is "give," just as in catching a baseball the hand is drawn back from the ball to lessen the impact.

"Cup" the blade over the puck (lean top edge of blade toward puck and bottom edge away) and glide blade along the ice.

The angle between the blade and the line of the pass should be 90 degrees. This helps prevent the puck from deflecting off the blade.

Again, hand position is important. A stickhandling position is very good because it presents a "soft stick" to control the puck after receiving the pass. However, lowering the low hand to passing position may be necessary to acquire adequate "firmness" to hold the pass, especially with young hockey players.

3. "GIVE" WITH STICK AS PUCK REACHES BLADE.

4. CUP STICK TO KEEP PUCK FROM BOUNCING OFF BLADE.

5. CONTROL PUCK FOR DRIBBLE, PASS OR SHOT.

shooting

Shooting is probably the most practiced of all fundamentals. This is partly due to the increase in popularity of the "slap shot." Young players love to slap the puck at the boards, and will do so for hours on end, often to the point of neglecting other fundamentals. There will always be players who "slap" the puck well but cannot shoot a wrist shot.

Wrist Shot

It is wise to learn the wrist shot well before spending much time on other shots. While the popular slap shot may be effective in some cases, there are many more situations in a game when one of the three other shots is best.

Shooting the puck is, in most cases, an attempt to score a goal. This leads to the single most important factor to stress: *Be sure the shot is on the goal!* When a player shoots, he should be thinking, "If nobody stops or deflects that one, it's in." All of the many books on goaltending written by goaltenders say the same thing. Goalies do not see more than half the pucks that score goals.

Shooting, more than the other fundamentals, depends on the player's physical maturity. Therefore, players probably will be at the intermediate or experienced levels before they master each shot.

Forehand Wrist Shot

Hands may be spread slightly more than in the passing or stickhandling positions, as much as two to three fists apart (12 to 15 inches).

To shoot the wrist shot, move the puck to the side of the body and behind the body line. This places the blade of the stick farther from the target than is the top of the shaft. The blade should be nearly at a right angle to the intended line of the shot.

Proper shooting action begins with both hands moving together toward the target while dragging the puck on the blade. How far the hands move forward usually is decided by the shooting motion. The puck should be positioned at about the middle of the blade or slightly forward of the middle. During the "dragging" motion the wrists should be cocked — back of the top hand toward the ice; palm of the lower hand toward the ice.

Shooting is a violent action. At the moment of the shot, the following occur in rapid succession, like an explosion. As the explosion begins, the top of the stick shaft should be nearer the target than the blade. The lower hand pushes forward quickly. The upper hand pulls back quickly. The lower wrist snaps forward and up, changing the hand's position from palm-to-ice to back-of-hand-to-ice. The upper wrist snaps forward and up, reversing the position of the hand from back-of-hand-to-ice to palm-to-ice.

To accomplish this push-pull, wrist-snapping action, exert full effort with hands and arms. Weight may be best utilized in the shooting action by driving off the inside foot (same side as puck) and striding to the outside foot.

Skating glide should "follow the shot." The follow-through with the stick usually will dictate the height of the shot: low follow-through, low shot; high follow-through, high shot.

Experienced players usually are able to look at the target as they shoot. With younger players, it is important that they look where they are shooting, but as in stickhandling, they might have more success with split vision, watching both the puck and the target.

1. BEGIN SHOT WELL TO REAR OF BODY.
2. DRIVE OFF REAR FOOT THEN TRANSFER WEIGHT TO FRONT FOOT. CONTINUE TO SKATE DURING SHOOTING ACTION.
3. PROJECT PUCK FORWARD WITH EXPLOSIVE SWEEPING MOTION AND GOOD WRIST ACTION.
4. FOLLOW THROUGH TO TARGET.

Backhand Wrist Shot

Most actions are similar to the forehand wrist shot. One exception is the starting position. It is very difficult to carry the puck on the backhand-shot side of the body and skate in a straight line toward the target. More often, the backhand shot comes off either a gliding or a crossover turn. Again, drag the puck forward and pull hard toward the target with the lower hand, in this case snapping the wrist from back-of-hand-to-ice to palm-to-ice. The top hand follows the lower hand (rather than opposing as in the forehand wrist shot), and the wrist snaps from palm-down to back-of-hand-down. Follow through with the stick low or high as demanded by the shot. Skating glide should follow the shot.

A final word about backhand shots: They are probably the least practiced but, according to some studies, the most effective. Goalies dislike backhand shots!

1. **START SHOT WELL TO REAR AND DRIVE OFF REAR FOOT.**
2. **TRANSFER WEIGHT TO SHOOT OFF FRONT FOOT.**
3. **KEEP STICK LOW AND FOLLOW THROUGH. CONTINUE TO SKATE.**

Snap Shot

This is a forehand shot "between" the wrist shot and the slap shot. It has the hitting-the-puck action of the slap shot (minus the long backswing) and the push-pull, wrist-snap action of the wrist shot. The shot can be made effectively with the puck in front of the body line (like the slap shot; unlike the wrist shot).

Hands should be in the same position as for a wrist shot — about 12 to 15 inches apart. While skating toward the net, the puck should be slightly in front of the body line. Draw the stick back about 12 to 18 inches. Swing down and forward hard, striking the ice about one inch behind the puck. As contact is made with the puck at the middle of the blade, repeat the push-pull, wrist-snap action of the wrist shot. As in the wrist shot, the height of the stick in the follow-through will do much to determine the height of the shot. Wrists must be kept very firm during this shot.

The snap shot can be made backhand following similar principles. However, a sweep wrist shot from the backhand side is likely to be more effective. A backhand snap shot is more of a "stab and hope" proposition.

1. **DRAW STICK BACK 12 TO 18 INCHES FROM PUCK.**
2. **SHOOT OFF FRONT FOOT AND SWING DOWN FORCEFULLY TO CONTACT ICE ABOUT ONE INCH BEHIND PUCK.**
3. **USE PUSH-PULL, WRIST-SNAP ACTION AS IN FOREHAND WRIST SHOT.**
4. **FOLLOW THROUGH TO TARGET.**

Flip Shot

This is a much neglected but very effective shot. At all levels, but particularly with young players, the ability to *flip* the puck often spells the difference between a goal or a shot into the goaltender.

Hands should be in the same position as with the wrist shot — about 12 to 15 inches apart. The shot usually is made from in front of the body line, with the puck on the blade more toward the toe than the middle. A good flip shot requires a sharp, quick wrist snap (as in the wrist shot), and a sharp, lifting action on the back edge (away from target) of the puck. The blade of the stick should be straight up and down or slightly open, rather than "cupped."

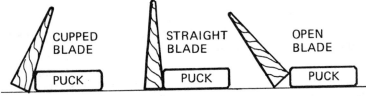

This shot can be especially useful during scrambles around the net. The shooter improves his scoring opportunity considerably by pulling the puck two or three feet back from the obstacle (often a fallen goalie) and quickly flipping it up and forward.

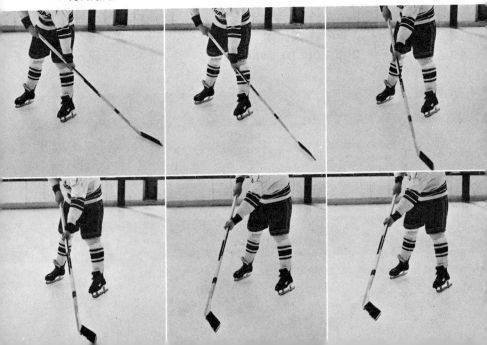

1. POSITION PUCK TOWARD TOE OF BLADE.
2. BLADE IS SLIGHTLY OPEN.
3. WITH QUICK SNAPPING MOTION OF WRISTS
   AND A LIFT ON BACK EDGE OF PUCK, FLIP PUCK
   OVER OPPONENT'S STICK OR FALLEN GOALTENDER.

Slap Shot

Poorly performed or used at the wrong times, the *slap shot* can be the source of considerable exasperation for both coach and player. However, the shot is so popular among young players that it is virtually impossible to ignore. Therefore, we include an explanation of the proper techniques.

As the stick is drawn back and up in an arc preparatory to the shot, the lower hand should slide down the shaft another 8 to 12 inches from the wrist-shot position. Weight of the body should shift to the leg away from the puck as the swing is started. Head should be approximately over the puck. Downswing of the stick should be a full-strength action. The blade should strike the ice one to two inches behind the puck, at about the middle (or slightly forward) of the blade. Watch the puck! The force of the swing ensures a certain amount of follow-through.

One of the defenses against the slap shot is to bodycheck the shooter while he is in the shooting action. Two factors make him vulnerable: He must look down at the puck and the follow-through position is not a strong balance position.

Obviously, because putting the puck into the net is the object of the game, shooting skill is very important. Be sure you work to improve these skills, but at the same time never forget that the end-over-ender that just barely gets over the red line counts the same as the shot that rips the back of the net and one more than the shot that just misses the corner and punches a hole in the boards!

1. *THINK* — IS THE SLAP SHOT THE *BEST* SHOT IN THIS SITUATION?

2. HANDS FAR APART ON BACKSWING.
   DRIVE OFF REAR FOOT.

3. HEAD IS OVER PUCK. KEEP EYES ON PUCK.

4. SHOOT OFF FRONT FOOT. STICK BLADE CONTACTS
   ICE BEHIND PUCK (ONE TO TWO INCHES).

5. KEEP STICK LOW AND FOLLOW THROUGH.

checking

If stickhandling is the single most important offensive skill, then checking is the most important defensive skill. Implicit in this statement is the realization that the skating ability of the players must be adequate for the level of competition.

There are three facets of checking:

1. Taking the puck away from an opponent (stickchecking).

2. Preventing an opponent from being in a favorable position to gain control of the puck (covering).

3. Taking the man away from the puck (bodychecking).

Stickchecking

Usually a player uses the blade of his stick to either "poke" or "hit" the puck off an opponent's stick or to "pull" the puck away from the opponent. Obviously, the checker is concentrating on the puck and very often he forgets the importance of (1) making sure he is under controlled speed and (2) maintaining body position on the opposing player; that is, coming at an angle toward the puck carrier rather than "straight on."

Players frequently stickcheck with only one hand on the stick. In this case, keep your stick arm well bent at the elbow so that as you close on the puck carrier you can "shoot" at the puck by extending your arm.

Many coaches, however, prefer to have their players stickcheck with both hands on the stick. The checker then is much closer to the puck carrier when he checks; should he miss the puck, he may have a good opportunity to bodycheck

The basic rule of defense: keep your body between the offensive player and your goal; as much as possible, "play the man." It should be emphasized that "playing the man" does not mean knocking him into tomorrow, but it does mean bumping him as safely and as often as you legally can. Remember, only the puck carrier or the last man to play the puck can be hit according to the rules. Hitting other people is interference.

Checking the puck away from a player by placing the shaft of the stick on the ice can be effective. This requires good position and timing.

To make a stickcheck, "fake" the puck carrier onto your top-hand side. Drop one hand (and usually knee) to the ice to place the shaft of the stick on the ice. Sweep forward toward the puck to stop the puck with your stick.

Performed well, the puck carrier loses the puck. Done poorly, the puck carrier has one less defensive player between him and the goal. (See p. 64.)

Covering

Covering is mainly skating to keep a defensive position between an opponent and the goal. This position is particularly important with backchecking.

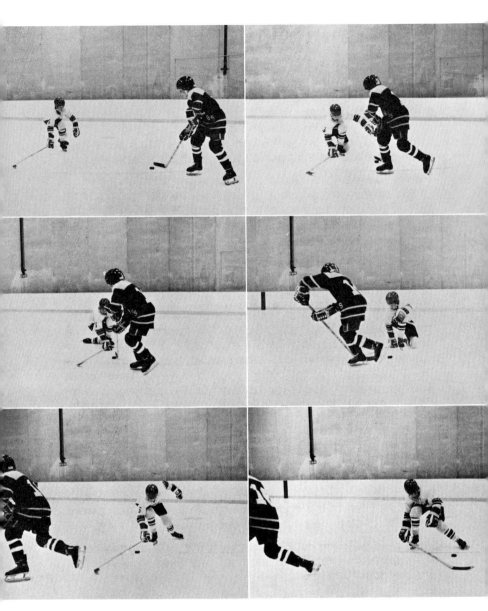

1. TO STICKCHECK, MANEUVER OPPONENT TO TOP-HAND SIDE.

2. DROP HAND AND KNEE, IF NECESSARY, TO PLACE BLADE ON ICE.

3. SWEEP FORWARD TOWARD PUCK TO FREE PUCK FROM OPPONENT.

Bodychecking

Hockey is a contact sport — and at times a collision sport. It is therefore important that players learn to bodycheck properly and within the rules and also to protect themselves as much as possible from injury caused by being bodychecked.

As in most contact sports, when a player is hit, his best defense is to "curl up" as compactly as possible. It is especially important that he drops his chin to his chest; in so doing, he pulls the back of his head to his body. His shoulders and shoulder pads then can absorb the impact of landing on the ice or colliding with the board. This action also "firms" the neck muscles so that the head doesn't snap back. Whenever possible, a player should try to reach out with his arms to cushion a collision with the boards, glass or screen.

When you know you are about to be bodychecked, reach out and place a hand on the player checking you. This often will cushion the blow and sometimes will allow you to slip off the check.

Two types of bodychecking usually are taught: (1) shoulder check and (2) hip check. While the techniques vary somewhat, there are factors common to both:

1. Try to hit when the opponent is not watching you or is not expecting to be hit. Many players like to "admire" their passes. This is great bodychecking time. Remember, however, that the check must be made *before* the pass is received by a teammate. A good "hitting time" is as the offensive player releases a slap shot.

2. Face to face. Straight-on checking is tough. It is better to get an angle or take advantage of a limited area; that is, an offensive player trying to go between a defensive player and the boards.

3. The checker must be under controlled speed, with knees well bent, to "create" the collision. On contact, the legs must provide a sudden thrust to propel the checker forward and into the opponent.

4. The checker must keep his eyes on the target — usually someplace between the chest and the waist.

Shoulder Check

In preparation for making a shoulder check as a defensive player, aim a shoulder at your opponent's chest to make contact with that shoulder and side of body.

Keep the free hand up to protect yourself or to push your opponent away should he see the check coming and move off the checking angle.

In making this check, establish a firm base with feet apart and weight on the inside edges of your skate blades. The knees are bent and with eyes on target your body is firm (coiled), ready to strike.

Remember, only two steps are permitted before hitting. But

Hip Check

The hip check is somewhat more difficult to make than the shoulder check since the timing must be so precise, coupled with the fact that the checker takes his eyes off the target just before impact.

The chance of success is greater when the offensive opponent is committed to a course which he cannot easily change.

As the defensive player, line up your opponent much as you would for a shoulder check. However, at the last moment, drop your head and shoulders to turn your hip into the stomach area of the offensive player.

upon contact, one leg should be well bent to provide a thrust forward and up, into the offensive player.

Resist the tendency to use your elbows when shoulder checking. Aside from the possibility of a penalty, elbows can cause severe injury.

1. ESTABLISH GOOD BASE POSITION WITH KNEES BENT.
2. AIM SHOULDER AT CHEST OF PLAYER.
3. LET OPPONENT SKATE INTO YOU. DON'T LUNGE!
4. UPON CONTACT, THRUST FORWARD AND UP WITH LEG OPPOSITE HITTING SHOULDER.

The leg closer to contact remains bent while the other leg extends sharply into a skating stride to thrust the hip farther into the opponent.

1. BE SURE OFFENSIVE OPPONENT IS "COMMITTED" TO HIS COURSE BEFORE ATTEMPTING HIP CHECK.
2. GLIDE INTO CHECKING LINE.
3. ESTABLISH SOLID BASE POSITION.
4. THRUST STRONGLY WITH LEG OPPOSITE HITTING HIP TO THROW THIS HIP AGAINST STOMACH OF OPPONENT.

Note about
Practicing Bodychecks

Practicing these checks is somewhat of a problem, because not too many players enjoy being on the receiving end.

At reduced speed, the offensive player skates a controlled course (along the blue line or between markers) and the defensive player makes contact without making the final, forceful thrust. As you gain confidence in your ability to hit and get hit, speed up the action. Eventually, you must hit at full speed if you are to learn this skill. One-on-one and one-on-two drills can be made into hitting practice if the defensemen do not use their sticks.

goaltending

Many hockey coaches believe that the goaltender is the most important player on the team. There can be no argument that your team is only as good as your goalie — he is the backbone of the team. Despite these facts, on most hockey teams the goaltender receives less formal coaching than any other player.

Remember, goaltending is a game within a game, and the most important quality of a goalie is that he must want to play in goal. In addition, the basic requirements are attitude, good eyesight, agility, coordination, good reflexes, courage, confidence and the right temperament.

Basic Stance

The feet should be about shoulder's width apart, with toes pointed slightly outward. The knees should be comfortably bent, with weight slightly forward. The upper part of the body should be bent forward at the waist. The head should be up, but relaxed on the neck. Arms should hang naturally on the outside of each knee; for freedom of movement, the arms are moved slightly in front of the body. The stick should be held somewhat loosely, but on the ice directly in front of the skates, leaving an "air cushion" of several inches between the toes of the skates and the back of the stick.

1. **BEND AT WAIST, KNEES FLEXED AND TOGETHER.**
2. **WEIGHT ON INSIDE EDGE OF SKATES.**
3. **PADS FORM INVERTED "V."**
4. **PLACE STICK BLADE FLAT UPON ICE THREE INCHES IN FRONT OF SKATES.**
5. **KEEP CATCHING GLOVE AWAY FROM BODY WITH WRIST COCKED.**

Basic Movements

A young goaltender should know how to make two types of sideward movement: (1) the short-distance move or "chop" steps and (2) the long-distance move.

Short Distance (Chop Steps)

This is for moving quickly to keep position in front of the puck. It is done by taking a short step without turning the foot (this allows goalie to always face forward; weight remains on the balls of the feet).

As a young goaltender progresses, he will make this step a sideways slide, always controlling the weight on the inside edge of the skate without turning his foot.

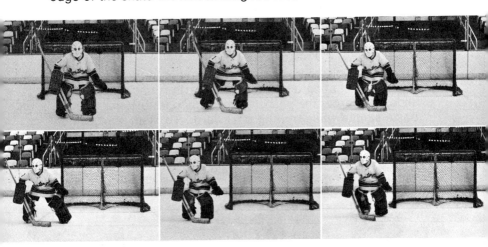

1. **TAKE SHORT STEPS WITHOUT TURNING YOUR FEET.**
2. **WITH PRACTICE, THE CHOP STEP BECOMES A SIDEWARD SLIDE-STEP.**
3. **ALWAYS CONTROL WEIGHT ON INSIDE EDGES OF SKATES.**

Long Distance

When the goalie is required to move sideways a long distance, he should turn his left toe outward (when moving left) and then push hard off the inside edge of the right skate. To stop, he turns his left foot toward the front, placing weight on the inside edge of the left foot.

Moving Forward and Back

To move quickly forward, push off the inside edge of one foot and glide in a basic stance toward the puck. To stop, use a "snowplow" stop with toes pointed in and weight on the inside edges of the skates.

To move quickly backward, push from the inside edge of one foot (as in skating backward). The farther back you wish to slide, the harder the push. (As much as possible, maintain the basic stance while moving backward.) To stop, place weight on the inside edges of the skates with toes slightly out.

Stopping the Puck
Use Your Body

It should be the ultimate objective of the goaltender to get his body in front of the puck on every shot. Since this is not always possible, glove, skate and stick saves also are used. However, if a young goalie starts with the idea of moving the body in front of all shots, he will find that his other options to make saves also improve.

To go backward an even greater distance, skate backward while maintaining as much as possible the basic stance.

1. **TO MOVE FORWARD PUSH OFF INSIDE EDGE OF ONE FOOT AND GLIDE TOWARD PUCK IN BASIC-STANCE POSITION.**
2. **USE "SNOWPLOW" STOP IF NECESSARY.**
3. **TO MOVE BACKWARD, AGAIN PUSH OFF ON INSIDE EDGE OF ONE SKATE. THE HARDER THE PUSH, THE LONGER THE GLIDE BACK.**

1. **ALWAYS ATTEMPT TO GET BODY IN FRONT OF PUCK.**
2. **REGARDLESS OF WHAT TYPE OF SAVE IS ATTEMPTED, BODY SERVES AS GOOD BACKUP.**

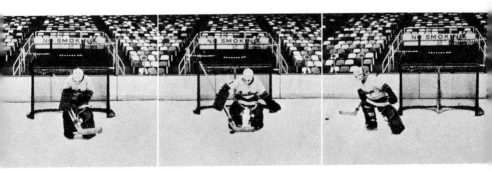

Glove Save

Hands are the best weapons for a goalie because they cover the greatest distance in the shortest time. Any shot that can be caught should be. When catching the puck, keep the wrist loose and flexible, and remember to keep the eyes on the puck. Shots to the stick side should be blocked with the back pad on the stick glove. The catching glove should be brought over to trap the puck against the back of the stick glove and thus prevent a rebound.

1. USE GLOVE AS IF CATCHING A BASEBALL.
2. CATCH PUCK AND BE READY TO THROW OR PASS TO TEAMMATE.
3. STAY ON FEET IN BASIC POSITION AS MUCH AS POSSIBLE.
4. CATCH ALL PUCKS TO GLOVE SIDE — EVEN THOSE WHICH WILL MISS THE NET — SO THAT YOU CAN CONTROL TO TEAMMATE.
5. STOP PUCK ON BACK OF STICK GLOVE (WAFFLE) AND TRAP PUCK WITH CATCHING GLOVE.

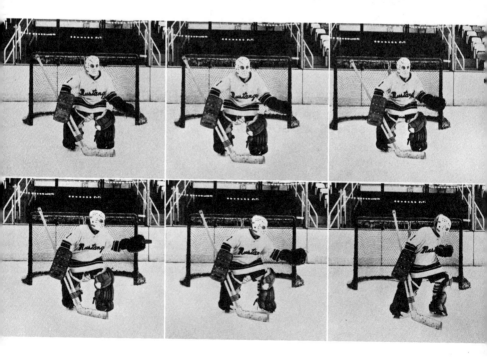

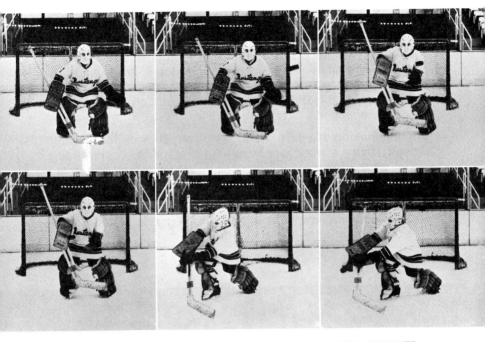

6. USE CATCHING GLOVE TO TRAP PUCK WHEN STOPPED BY BODY OR PADS TO PREVENT REBOUND.

Skate Save

To make a skate save with the right foot, push off the inside edge of the left skate, turning the right toe to the outside so that the puck will hit the inside edge of the right skate blade. This should deflect the puck to the corner. Left-skate save is just the opposite.

When making this save, try to keep your stick on the ice and push it in the same direction as your skate. Keep your pushing foot on the ice as long as possible, and return to the basic stance as soon as you can.

The leg pads are used mainly for blocking the angle to the net, but also to stop low shots directly at the goalie, and low "corner" shots that are just above the stick but too low to catch.

SKATE SAVE

LEG SAVE

1. PROJECT WEIGHT OVER EXTENDED KNEE.

2. ANGLE SKATE BLADE TO SIDE WITH SLIGHT ARC. KEEP BLADE ON ICE.

3. WATCH PUCK CONTACT SKATE.

4. DEFLECT PUCK WITH SKATE. WHEN POSSIBLE, USE STICK AS BACKUP.

5. ON LOW CORNER SHOTS, USE LEG PAD AND SKATE-SAVE TECHNIQUES TO DEFLECT PUCK TO CORNER.

6. EYES ON PUCK — ALWAYS.

Stick Save

A youth goalie should use as long a stick as can be controlled well — full size, if possible.

The stick is held loosely but with control, usually just above the wide portion of the shaft. The grip tightens in making a play.

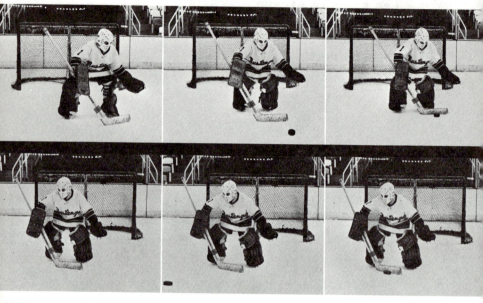

4. SOMETIMES IT IS NECESSARY TO FREEZE PUCK WITH GLOVE.

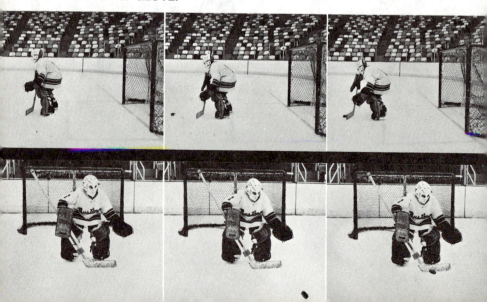

The stick is used for stopping the puck (particularly low shots), clearing, poke checking and intercepting passes.

1. **MAKE SURE STICK IS PERPENDICULAR TO ICE SO PUCK DOESN'T SLIDE UP AND OVER.**
2. **BLOCK PUCK WITH STICK.**
3. **DEFLECT PUCK TO SIDE.**

5. **LAY STICK BLADE IN FRONT OF GLOVE TO PREVENT OPPONENT FROM POKING PUCK LOOSE.**

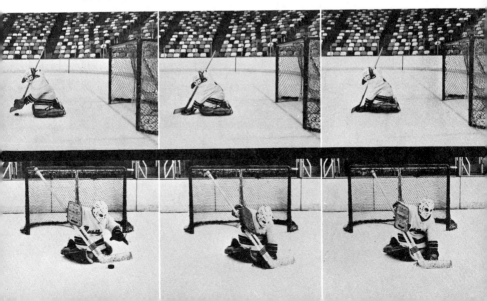

Two-Leg Slide Save

The "stacking pads" save is done much the same as hook sliding in baseball. To stack to his left, the goalie must slide to his left, tucking his right foot and leg behind his left leg. He then slides down on his right hip, and as it makes contact with the ice, he kicks the right foot and leg forward. This kicking action "stacks" the pads one on top of the other. It is important that the puck be within four feet of the goalie when he starts the stacking action. Generally, stacking is a desperation move.

1. **PUCK SHOULD BE WITHIN FOUR FEET OF GOALIE.**
2. **TIMING IS MOST IMPORTANT SINCE PUCK IS AT SHORT RANGE.**
3. **MAKE SMOOTH, CONTINUOUS MOTION, LANDING ON ONE SIDE AND EXTENDING ENTIRE BODY UPON ICE. AVOID HOPPING BEFORE MAKING MOVE. EXTEND GLOVE HAND UPWARD FROM BODY.**
4. **STICK SHOULD BE FLAT, READY TO HOOK PUCK INTO BODY TO PREVENT REBOUND IF POSSIBLE.**

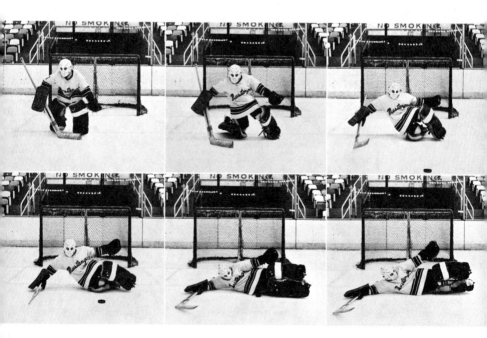

V-Drop Save

This move is used against a "deking" forward. The goaltender moves out in front of the crease and drops to the inside of his knees and legs, thus fanning his feet out so that the toes point toward the posts of the goal. This places the pads in a "V" position, completely covering the surface of the ice.

The secret of this move is to keep the chest and upper body lined up with the puck, enabling the goalie to use his gloves and chest to make the save should the shooter flip the puck over the pads. Again, the puck must be within four feet of the goalie, for this is another desperation move. A common fault is that the goalie gets "caught up" with the motion of the shooter rather than staying between the puck and the goal.

1. KEEP CHEST AND UPPER BODY LINED UP WITH PUCK.
2. MAKE DROP WITH PUCK IN SHORT RANGE.
3. BE READY TO "POP" BACK ONTO FEET.

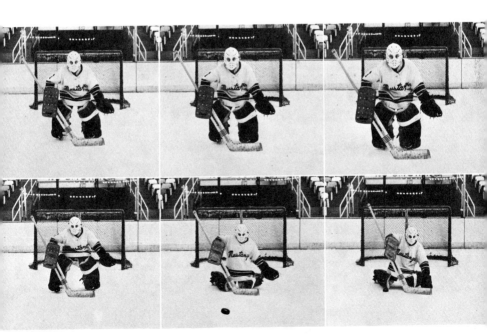

Play the Angles

The single most important skill in stopping the puck is learning to play the angles, which is 70 percent or more of goaltending. Quickness is a great asset, but the goalie also must be in the right position to make the save.

There are three rules to remember about playing the angles: (1) Cut down the shooter's vision of the net, (2) never "give" the shooter the short side and (3) play the puck, not the shooter's body.

On shots from the extreme side of the rink, one skate and the upper body should rest against the post. If the play develops in front of the net, edge away from the post to face the puck squarely.

1. **KEEP STICK BLADE IN FRONT OF SKATES.**
2. **FACE PUCK SQUARELY, NOT SHOOTER.**
3. **MOVE IN ARC FOLLOWING PUCK ACROSS ICE.**
4. **USE BACK OF CATCHING GLOVE AND HANDLE OF STICK TO FIND POSTS AND POSITION YOURSELF WITHOUT TAKING EYES OFF PUCK.**
5. **"TELESCOPE" OUT FROM THE ARC WHEN CARRIER PREPARES TO SHOOT.**

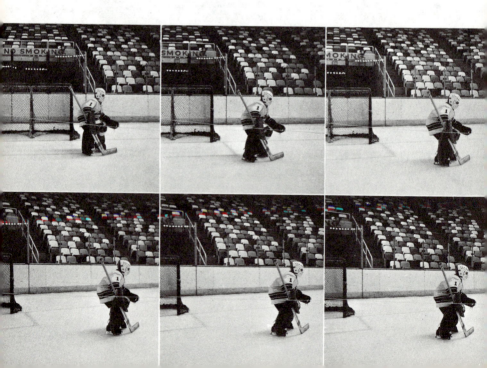

Breakaway

An opponent with the puck bearing down on the goalie un-challenged by a defenseman presents a special problem for the goalie.

On a breakaway, face the puck squarely. Stay at the edge of the goal crease with front of skates on crease line as long as carrier has puck in front of him in a stickhandling position. Move out to cut down the angle as soon as carrier prepares to shoot.

Let carrier make the first move. Use a two-leg slide if opponent attempts to deke. One thing to remember — most forwards have a tendency to go to the backhand when attempting to fake a goalie out of position.

Control of Rebounds

The difference between a good and a great goalie is the ability to control rebounds. Most goals are scored on rebounds, tip-ins and screen shots.

To control rebounds a goalie should:

- Use a "dead pad." Cushion puck to fall at feet.
- Trap puck against body or in equipment.
- Give with the stick to "cushion" a soft rebound.
- Smother every loose puck which cannot be cleared.

Six Rules of Goaltending:

- Watch the puck.
- Don't commit yourself too soon.
- Cut down the shooting angle.
- Stay on your feet.
- Get equipment blockage behind all shots.
- "Talk it up" in goal.

The Rink

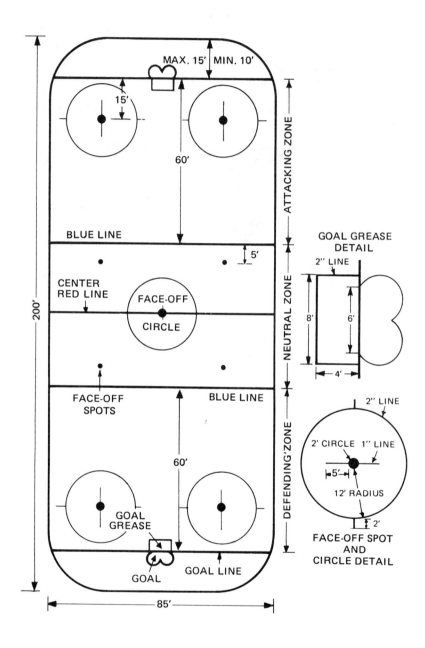

MAX. 15' MIN. 10'

15'

60'

BLUE LINE

ATTACKING ZONE

CENTER
RED LINE

FACE-OFF

CIRCLE

NEUTRAL ZONE

5'

200'

FACE-OFF
SPOTS

BLUE LINE

60'

GOAL
GREASE

DEFENDING ZONE

GOAL

GOAL LINE

85'

GOAL GREASE
DETAIL

2" LINE

8'

6'

4'

2" LINE

2' CIRCLE 1" LINE

5'

12' RADIUS

2'

FACE-OFF SPOT
AND
CIRCLE DETAIL

rules simplified
The Rink

The game of ice hockey is played on an ice surface known as a *rink*. The recommended size of the rink is 200 feet long and 85 feet wide with the corners rounded off in the arc of a circle with a radius of 28 feet.

The rink is enclosed by a wooden fence or wall known as the *boards* which should extend in height not less than 40 inches nor more than 48 inches above the ice. The boards' surface should be white in color. All doors giving access to the rink must open away from the ice.

The Ice Markings

Ten feet from each end of the rink a red line, two inches wide, is drawn completely across the width of the ice and continued vertically up the side of the boards. This is called the *goal line*. Regulation goal posts and nets are set in a manner to remain stationary during the progress of a game. Goal posts should extend four feet above the surface of the ice and be set six feet apart measured from inside the posts. A crossbar connects goal posts. Attached to the goal frame at either end of the rink is a net, draped so as to prevent the puck's coming to rest outside.

The area immediately in front of each goal is called the *goal crease*. The goal crease is laid out as follows: one foot from the outside of each goal post, lines four feet in length and two inches in width are drawn at right angles to the goal line and the points of these lines farthest from the goal are joined by another line, two inches in width.

The goal crease area includes all space outlined by the crease lines and the area extending four feet vertically to the level of the top of the goal frame.

The Zones

The playing area between the two goals is divided into three sections by lines 12 inches in width and blue in color. These *blue lines* are drawn 60 feet out from the goals, extending parallel with the goal lines and continuing vertically up the side of the boards.

That portion of the ice surface in which the goal is situated is called the *defending zone* of the team defending that goal. The center portion is known as the *neutral zone* and that section farthest from the defended goal is the team's *attacking zone.*

A red line, 12 inches wide, crosses the rink at center ice parallel with the goal lines and continues up the side of the boards. This line is called the *center line.* This line is not used in games played under NCAA rules.

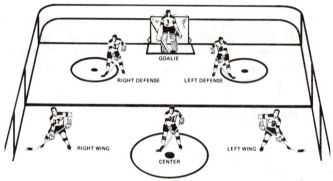

The Team

A team is comprised of six players — one center, two wingmen, two defensemen and one goalkeeper (also known as a goaltender or "goalie").

Equipment

Sticks may not be longer than 55 inches with blades no wider than three inches nor less than two inches. The goalkeeper's blade may be 3½ inches wide. The curve of the blade can be no greater than one-half inch.

Skates must be of approved design and equipped with safety heel tips. Use of speed skates, fancy skates or any skates so designed as possibly to cause injury is prohibited.

All protective equipment must be worn in such a way as not to cause injury to other players. All protective gear must be worn in the prescribed manner; that is, helmets buckled, mouthguards in place.

The Puck

The puck is one inch thick, three inches in diameter and weighs between 5½ and six ounces.

About the Game

The game is played in three, generally 20-minute, periods. The time of the periods is adjusted for the various age classifications.

Start of Game and Periods

Each period shall begin with a face-off in the center of the rink.

Players facing off stand squarely facing opponent's end of the rink approximately one stick length apart with stick blades on the ice. Players must have one skate on each side of the line running through the face-off spot and behind the line parallel to the goal line. No other player is allowed to enter the face-off circle or be within 15 feet of the players facing off. Any violations require another face-off.

Substitution

Substitutions may be made while play is in progress provided that the player coming off the ice is at the players' bench and out of play before the substituting player enters the rink.

Goals and Assists

A goal is scored when the puck enters the goal from the stick of a player of the attacking side. The puck must be completely across the goal line. If any part of the puck is touching the goal line it is not a valid goal.

The scoring of a goal is credited to the player who propels the puck into the opponent's goal. Each goal counts one point in the player's record.

When a goal is scored, an "assist" may be credited to the player or players, not more than two, taking part in the play immediately preceding the goal. An assist also counts one point in the player's record.

Offside Blue Line

The puck must precede the players of the attacking team across the blue line of their opponent's defensive zone.

Offside Pass

AHAUS rules provide that the puck may be passed by a player to a teammate within any one of the three zones. A player may not, however, pass the puck from his defensive zone to a teammate who is beyond the center red line. If the puck precedes the player across the line, there is no violation of this rule.

The position of the player's skates is the determining factor in calling an offside pass violation. The player is considered onside if any part of either skate is behind or touching the center red line.

Icing

Icing the puck shall be called if a player shoots the puck from behind the center red line across his opponent's goal line. "Icing" occurs the moment the puck crosses the goal line unless it enters the goal or passes through the goal crease.

Icing Is Not Called When:

- An opposing player touches or has a chance to play the puck before it crosses the goal line.

- The team of the player shooting the puck is short-handed because of a penalty.

- An attacking player who is not offside touches the puck before it crosses the goal line.

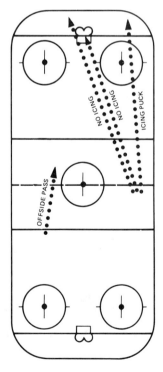

Playing the Puck

The puck must be advanced at all times. Except to carry the puck behind its goal once, a team with possession of the puck in its defensive zone must advance the puck toward the opposing goal unless prevented from doing so by an opposing player. For a violation of this rule a face-off shall take place at a spot adjacent to the goal of the team causing the delay. If the puck goes outside the rink or strikes any obstacles above the playing surface other than the boards, glass or screen, the face-off takes place where it was last played, except if it was last touched by an attacking player in his attacking zone. In this case the face-off shall be in the neutral zone.

If the puck is tied up between two opposing players, the face-off will take place at the nearest point to where the stoppage occurred.

A player, except the goalkeeper, may not close his hand on the puck; for such an infraction a minor penalty is imposed. Any player other than the goalkeeper who deliberately falls upon the puck or gathers it into his body shall be subject to a minor penalty.

Officials

There are two systems of officiating. The three-man system is made up of one referee and two linesmen and the two-man is composed of two referees.

The "off-ice" officials consist of a game timekeeper, a penalty timekeeper, an official scorer and two goal judges.

Penalties*

Minor Penalty
The player is ruled off the ice for a period of two minutes. A substitute is not permitted.

Major Penalty
The player is ruled off the ice for a period of five minutes. A substitute is not permitted unless the "coincident major penalties" rule applies.

*Penalty times are adjusted in relation to the length of the periods in youth games.

Match Penalty

The player is ruled out for the balance of the game. A team-mate shall take his place on the penalty bench to serve the five- or ten-minute time penalty depending on the rule for which the match penalty was imposed.

Game Misconduct

The player is suspended from the balance of the game. An immediate substitute is permitted.

Misconduct Penalty

This involves the removal of a player from the game for a period of ten minutes. A teammate is permitted to replace the penalized player.

Goalkeeper Penalties

When a minor, major or misconduct penalty is imposed on a goaltender, the time penalty shall be served by a teammate on the ice at the time the penalty is imposed.

Penalty Shot

The puck shall be placed on the center face-off spot. All the players of both teams shall be at their respective players' bench. Only the goalkeeper may defend against a penalty shot. The player taking the penalty shot may skate in any direction except that once he crosses the blue line he must proceed directly toward the goal. The goalkeeper must remain in the goal crease until the player taking the penalty shot has touched the puck. The player is allowed to take one shot and may not play a rebound from the goalkeeper, goal or backboards. Once the puck has crossed the goal line the penalty shot is completed.

While there are several violations for which a penalty shot may be awarded, the most common of these is when an offensive player, with no other opponent to pass other than the goalkeeper, is fouled from behind.

Common Infractions

Abuse of Officials

A misconduct penalty shall be imposed on any player who uses obscene, profane or abusive language directed toward any game official. A bench minor penalty may be imposed if any player, trainer, coach, manager or club executive on the players' bench uses abusive language.

Attempt to Injure or Deliberate Injury

A match penalty shall be imposed on any player who injures or attempts to injure an opponent or official.

Boarding

A minor or major penalty, at the discretion of the referee, shall be imposed on any player who bodychecks, cross-checks, elbows, charges or trips an opponent in such a manner as to cause him to be thrown violently into the boards.

Charging

A minor or major penalty shall be imposed on a player who runs, jumps into or charges an opponent.

Cross-Checking

At the discretion of the referee, a minor or major penalty shall be imposed on a player who cross-checks an opponent. A *cross-check* shall mean a check delivered with both hands on the stick without any part of the stick touching the ice.

Elbowing and Kneeing

A minor penalty shall be imposed on any player who checks an opponent with his elbow or knee.

Falling on Puck

A minor penalty shall be imposed on a player other than the goalkeeper who deliberately falls on or gathers a puck into his body.

Fisticuffs

At the discretion of the referee, a minor, double minor or major penalty shall be assessed for fisticuffs. A player who incurs a major penalty for fisticuffs shall also receive an automatic game misconduct.

High Sticking

Carrying of sticks above the normal shoulder height is prohibited. A minor or major penalty shall be imposed on any player violating this rule, at the discretion of the referee.

Holding

A minor penalty shall be imposed on a player who holds an opponent with hands, stick or in any other way.

Hooking

A minor penalty shall be imposed on a player who impedes or seeks to impede the progress of an opponent by hooking him with the stick.

Interference

A minor penalty shall be imposed on a player who bodychecks or impedes the progress of an opponent who is not in possession of the puck.

Kicking

A match penalty shall be imposed on any player who kicks or attempts to kick another player. A substitute is permitted after five or ten minutes at the discretion of the referee.

Slashing

At the discretion of the referee, a minor or major penalty shall be imposed against a player who slashes or attempts to slash an opponent.

Spearing or Butt-Ending

A minor or major penalty, at the discretion of the referee, plus an automatic misconduct shall be imposed against a player who spears or butt-ends or attempts to spear or butt-end an opponent.

Tripping

A minor penalty shall be imposed on any player who positions his stick, knee, foot, arm or elbow in such a manner as to cause an opponent to trip or fall.

Key to Diagrams

→ . . . . SKATING DIRECTION

〜〜〜► . . . . SKATING WITH PUCK

● ● ● ● ● ● ● ●► . . . . PASS

– – – – – – – ► . . . . SHOT ON GOAL

☒ . . . . TEAM OFFENSIVE PLAYER

Ⓧ . . . . TEAM DEFENSIVE PLAYER

■ . . . . BLOCKS

● . . . . PUCK

team play

Beginning hockey players soon figure out that offense means getting in goal-scoring position and, in fact, scoring goals. Defense means stopping the offense and recovering the puck. This simple assessment is sufficient to play the game. However, after learning why certain things happen on the ice, players must learn to *create* situations rather than just let them happen.

Most young hockey players, if left alone, will fall into the "swarm" system — or nonsystem, if you prefer — of offense and defense; that is, everybody goes where the puck is. If, however, you can get organized just a little, you can achieve greater results.

"Position" Offense

The basic, or simplest, offensive pattern is "everybody play his position." This is a concept that should be learned from the beginning. In simple terms — spread out! The left wing skates up and down his side of the rink, the right wing up and down his side and so on. This creates a territorial division of the ice surface (see illustrations). If you will maintain these lanes or areas and do one more thing — pass the puck to the open man — you will have a reasonably acceptable offensive system.

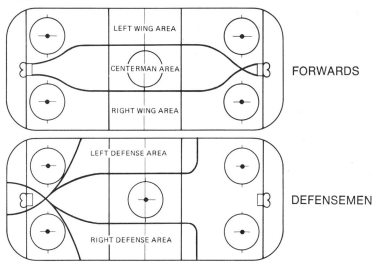

"Territorial" Defense

The simplest of team defenses — and one that is complementary to "position" offense — is defensive assignments by territory (see illustration).

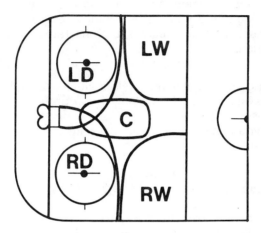

The wings must backcheck the offensive wings, but once in the defensive zone, the wings will usually cover the offensive "pointmen" (usually the offensive team's defensemen).

The preceding is team offense and defense at their simplest; once mastered, teams can move on to more complicated offensive and defensive patterns.

Following are some relatively basic offensive patterns and defensive assignments that may be used by teams at all levels.

First, a few introductory comments. In a competitive game, it would be foolish for the defensive team to think it could stop the offense from getting a shot (or shots) on goal. Normally, the offensive team will get 25 to 30 shots on goal. By playing well, the defense may limit the offense to fewer than 20 shots, but it is suggested that a more realistic objective is for the defense to work toward forcing the offense to take poorer shots on goal. Conversely, the offense should try to increase its shots on goal, but — more important — try to get *better* shots.

The Numbers Game

There are several offense versus defense situations a coach can consider and try to deal with. Like so many things, hockey becomes a game of numbers:

1. One offensive player against the goalie, while most desirable from the offensive standpoint, is totally unacceptable for the defensive team.

2. One offensive player against one defensive player (assume the goalie is in position) is the most frequently occurring situation in a hockey game. ("Thee against me, Friend, and we are going to come to a decision!") Rather than tie that decision to "goal-no goal," it may be helpful to consider a good shot on goal as a victory for the offense and a poor shot (or no shot) on goal as a victory for the defense.

Using these measures of success, the thinking of the offensive player must then be something like this: "If I can fake him (the defensive player) to the outside and cut inside him, I'll get a good shot on goal." The defensive player thinks, "If I can keep him (the offensive player) to the outside, the best he can do is get a poor-angle shot."

For the offensive player to be successful, he must stickhandle well, including faking, and control his skating (balance, power and speed). The defensive player must maintain a position between the offensive player and the goal and *force* the offensive player to the outside.

Defensive Player Rule

In the one-on-one situations, play the man, *not* the puck. (*Playing the man* does not mean draping him over the flag; it does mean keeping your body between the offensive player and your goal and making body contact as necessary, usually at about 12 to 18 feet from the goal.)

It is just as important for the offensive player to know this rule as it is for the defensive player. If the defensive player follows the rule (assuming comparable skill levels of players), the defense will "win" more often — perhaps as high as 70 to 80 percent of the time.

The offensive player has two things going for him in a one-on-one situation: (1) He knows where he wants to go *before* he goes and therefore may confuse the defensive player with fakes, changes of speed and so on and (2) the defensive player, being human, would really like to "get" the offensive player, and better still, get the puck. The offensive player's aim should be to force the defensive player to commit himself *first*.

It is also important for the offensive player to know that defensive players (in this case defensemen), are "comfortable" near the slot and the defensive alley but uncomfortable the farther away from this area they must move (see illustration).

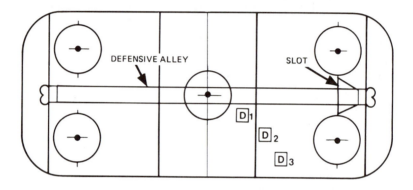

D_1 — "At home."
D_2 — Not too happy being here, would like to return "home." Also begins to wonder if his defensive partner is "covering" for him.
D_3 — Unless he has control of the puck, he is very uncomfortable this far from "home."

Two Situations

In addition to one-on-one, coaches normally consider two-on-one, two-on-two, three-on-two, three-on-three and so on up to five-on-five. We suggest that you consider only two situations — *one-on-one* and *two-on-one*. If more than one offensive player is in position to attack the offensive zone, only two should combine at one time, and their goal should be to attack or isolate one defensive player. The two offensive players are in control of the puck; therefore, they should be able to go where they want to go. Thus, for example, the two offensive players could attack the *right side* of the offensive zone, isolating the left defenseman. If the right defenseman chooses to help he must leave his "comfort zone" to create equal numerical strength of two-on-two.

Move around the ice trying to create two-on-one situations, forcing the defense to move players from normal defensive positions ("comfortable" places) to provide equal numerical strength. When the defense adjusts, the puck carrier then has three options:

1. Attack his defensive man one-on-one.
2. Carry the puck to create a new two-on-one situation with a different teammate.
3. Pass the puck to a teammate who can create a new two-on-one situation.

Obviously, all of this is much easier to write about than to do. However, if the offensive team persists in trying to create two-on-one situations, it can be successful primarily because of two basic defensive considerations: (1) Defensemen do not like to be out of position (for example, left defensemen like to stay on the left side, right defensemen on the right) and (2) more times than not, somebody (one of the forwards) does not backcheck hard enough or soon enough.

Team Offense

The first question players must resolve is, "When are we on offense?" The offense-or-defense question centers on control of the puck. Team puck control falls into three categories:

1. We have it — we are on *offense.*
2. They have it — we are on *defense.*
3. Nobody has it (loose puck). This is the condition that the game is all about: *If* we win the race to the loose puck, we go on offense. The trouble, as all players quickly learn, is *if.*

The safest way — from an offense-or-defense standpoint — to resolve the dilemma: We are on offense when we control the puck; at all other times we are on defense. This should put your team into a defensive pattern when you go after loose pucks.

It is worth noting here that the team which wins the race for loose pucks usually wins the game. Be sure to skate hard for the loose pucks.

The object of team offense is to control the puck long enough and well enough to get a good shot on goal. Here are some simple offensive patterns for the three zones:

Offense in the Defensive Zone

Offense in your own zone is commonly referred to as a "breakout" pattern. Your team should move the puck quickly and safely out of your defensive zone and into the middle zone. For the purposes of developing and drilling on this pattern, we usually assume recovery of the puck by a defenseman. The wings go quickly to the breakout zones. The center first goes away from the "puck side" of the zone, then skates across the puck side. The defenseman has the following options open to him:

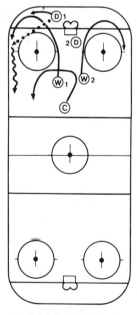

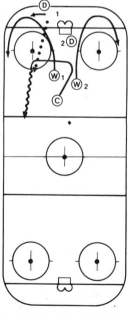

1. PASS TO WING.   2. PASS TO CENTER.

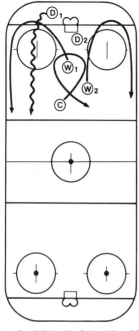 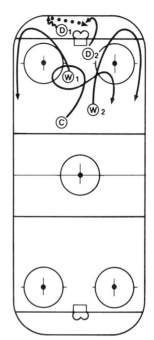

3. CARRY PUCK UP ICE.

4. PASS TO **D₂** (**D₁** NEEDS TO "CALL" **D₂** TO ARRANGE THIS OPTION).

D₁ also could move behind the net and set up the same options on the opposite side.

In Option 1, **W₁**, after receiving the initial pass, can (a) pass to **C**, (b) carry puck, (c) return a back pass to **D₁**. Passing from **W₁** to **W₂** or **D₂** usually is risky.

Offense in the Middle Zone

Usually this zone is not used much for offensive play. It is jammed between "thank goodness we got out of our zone" and "how can I get free in front of the net?" Bearing in mind the previous discussion about creating a two-on-one situation, the middle zone should be used to start this action. In this zone, players should be able to "read" which side lacks backchecking. They should then move to attack the defenseman on that side and move him away from his defensive alley.

Therefore, we suggest that the puck carrier enter the offensive zone near the boards.

This situation is usually referred to as three-on-two. Moving the puck to **W₂** provides the opportunity to make it two-on-one, and forces **D₁** to make a decision: Does he want to stay one-on-one with **W₁** or should he move over to help **D₂** and thus leave "his side" open? Even if **W₁** is covered by backchecking, **D₁** will wonder about leaving his side. "Can I really trust Billy Backcheck to stay with that guy all the way?"

By isolating one defensive player in a two-on-one situation, you put tremendous pressure on him physically and you "provide the opportunity" for him *and his teammates* to make mental errors.

If it is all this easy, one wonders why scores are not 98-97. The offensive players also have a few problems to contend with: (1) poor stickhandling skills (lose the puck), (2) poor passing skills (miss a pass) and (3) poor skating skills (lose speed or power or fall down). If the defense just stood still, the offense would likely win (get a good shot on goal) only about 70 or 80 percent of the time. And, of course, the goalie would stop some of those shots.

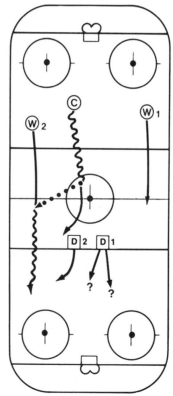

Offense in the Offensive Zone

One way of playing offensive zone hockey is to "throw it in and chase it; somebody will make a mistake!" This theory is supported by some success. However, it doesn't seem to make much sense to play your heart out on defense to gain control of the puck and then shoot it away (admittedly into the offensive zone) and try to get it back again.

As a last resort, when no one on your team is free, "shooting it in" may be the best alternative. However, players should have an *orderly* method for entering the offensive zone, one that gives at least an opportunity to control the defense.

You can build a relatively simple offensive zone system out of very basic moves. These patterns are limited only by the imagination of the coach and players and by the skill level of the players. (If your team cannot skate from position A to B without falling down, we suggest that you spend no time developing an offensive pattern and considerable time on skating skills.)

The following is an approach to developing an offensive pattern:

1. We will work to get two-on-one situations.
2. We will enter the offensive zone near the boards.
3. The wings will try to "cut" one of three basic patterns: **A** — belly curve, **B** — break, **C** — inside cut (see illustration).

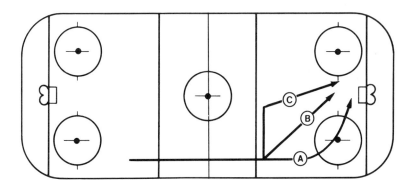

4. We will try to set up one of the following options:

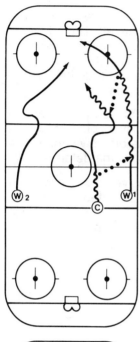

Back Pass

1. **C** passes to **W₁** about at the red line.
2. **W₁** carries wide, beats the defenseman on a belly curve if possible or makes a back pass to **C**.
3. **W₁** continues to move through entire pattern.
4. **W₂** enters zone, hesitates to let **W₁** and **C** develop pattern. When pass is made back, **W₂** *breaks* for net.
5. **C**, after pass to **W₁**, skates forward across the blue line, then cuts behind **W₁** (about 15 feet back and 5 feet inside **W₁**).
6. When **C** receives the back pass, he may pass to **W₁** or **W₂** or skate in and shoot.

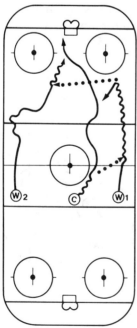

Wing Set

1. Same as Option 1 (Back Pass) until **W₁** gets to top of face-off circle; here **W₁** *stops.*
2. **C** breaks for net.
3. **W₂** makes inside cut across the blue line and up the center (slot).
4. **W₁** passes to **W₂**.
5. **W₁** moves behind **W₂** as a safety measure.

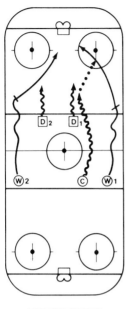

Center Set

1. When defensemen back over blue line, center carries puck toward *one* defenseman, gets over blue line and *stops.*
2. If defenseman moves toward **C**, **C** passes to **W**$_1$ or **W**$_2$ (both on break patterns).
3. If defenseman moves back, **C** carries in and shoots.

Key to Diagrams
p. 92

Double Back Pass

1. This requires agreement by the forward line that on a specific rush (first time, every time this shift and so on) they will play for a double back pass.
2. Same as Option 1 (Back Pass) except **W**$_2$ moves across the ice and accepts second back pass from **C**.

Developing a team offense can provide great satisfaction — and great frustration. Be sure you understand that as long as you try to make patterns work, you should not be disturbed by lack of success. If one in ten works very well, that's good. As players become more skillful, two or three in ten may be a good level of success.

Team Defense

The two words that best describe team defense are *hard work.* Boys generally like to play offense but have a very difficult time putting forth the effort necessary to make a team defense work well.

Going back to the discussion of hockey by the numbers, if everybody on defense does his job, defense should be no worse than one-on-one times five. The three major problems that cause this to break down are: (1) Somebody does not stay one-on-one (for example, a forechecker does not backcheck *now*), (2) a more highly skilled offensive player beats a less highly skilled defensive player or (3) the offense has the advantage of knowing where it is going, how it will get there, and when. In each of these cases, the defense adjusts and someone tries to "help out" (which is a must), but usually in doing so makes it possible for the offense to create a desired two-on-one situation.

There are three conditions of numbers with which the defense should be concerned:

1. Even (one-on-one) — play the *man.*

2. More offensive players than defensive players (two-on-one) — play the puck situation. Play close to the defensive alley, thus encouraging the offense to go outside to try to get to the goal. In this situation, the defensive player should (a) try to gain time so that a teammate can get back to help or (b) give up a poor shot on goal. Above all, don't let the two offensive players get the puck into the slot.

3. More defensive players than offensive players (one-on-two) — a good time to bodycheck the offensive player. One defender plays the man while the other takes the puck.

Defensive patterns usually are based on the type of forechecking a team will use and the type of coverage it will have in its own (defensive) zone. It usually is assumed (frequently too optimistically) that both offensive wings will be covered by backcheckers.

Forechecking

You may wish to consider a method of designating the player or players who are to forecheck. For example, you can *center only* forecheck; this should mean that if the center is not able to forecheck, you do not forecheck. You also may say that the *closest man* forechecks. This method gives you the potential of later debates about who really was the closest, but it does ensure forechecking.

Regardless of the system or the number of players forechecking, position should be stressed at all times. The forechecker should always "get an angle" on the puck carrier so, at the very least, he can confine the offensive player's movement to one side of the ice. In other words, never forecheck straight at the puck carrier.

One-Man Forechecking

The forechecker must turn the puck carrier, forcing him to the side. Wings of the offensive team must be covered. The defenseman (pointman) on the puck side stays in the zone as long as possible.

1. **SKATE COURSE AT SUCH AN ANGLE AS TO TURN PUCK CARRIER INTO CORNER OR SIDE BOARDS.**
2. **KEEP PUCK CARRIER IN LINE WITH YOU.**
3. **CONTINUE TO CLOSE SPACE BETWEEN YOU, THE CARRIER AND THE BOARDS.**
4. **PINCH CARRIER INTO BOARDS.**

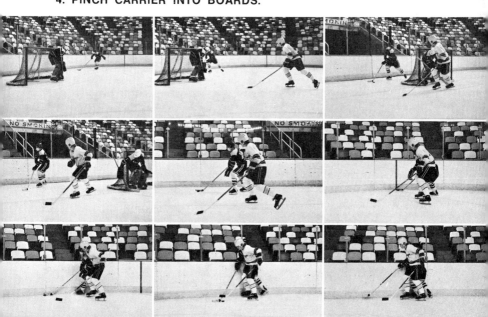

The purpose of this forechecking pattern is to make the offensive wings unavailable to bring the puck out of the defensive zone. The forechecker tries to take the puck away, to force the offensive player to carry the puck up the side and into the pointman, to make a bad pass, or to use his defensemen to break out.

A highly skilled forechecker will get the puck occasionally, but the offensive team should be able to beat one forechecker by using the three open players to move the puck out.

Two-Man Forechecking

For this example, the center and the puck-side wing are the two forecheckers. Two-man forechecking is most successful when the puck carrier is back of an imaginary line across the top of the face-off circles (cross-hatched area).

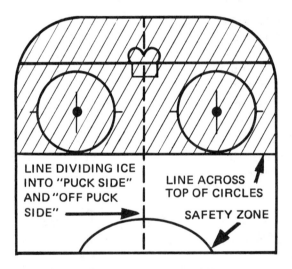

LINE DIVIDING ICE INTO "PUCK SIDE" AND "OFF PUCK SIDE"

LINE ACROSS TOP OF CIRCLES

SAFETY ZONE

1. **LEAD CHECKER CONTROLS PUCK CARRIER, TURNING HIM INTO CORNER OF BOARDS.**

2. **SECOND FORECHECKER STAYS BACK SIX TO EIGHT FEET UNTIL PUCK CARRIER IS CONTROLLED.**

3. **SECOND FORECHECKER MOVES IN TO BODYCHECK PUCK CARRIER.**

4. **IF LEAD FORECHECKER CANNOT BUMP PUCK CARRIER, HE SHOULD AT LEAST CONTROL HIS PATHWAY UNTIL SECOND FORECHECKER CAN MAKE CONTACT.**

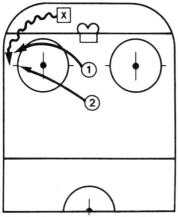

#**1** angles puck carrier to corner and tries to bump him.

#**2** moves in for puck.

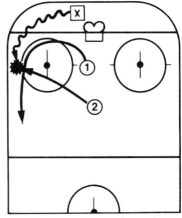

#**1** controls path of puck carrier.

#**2** cuts or rolls puck carrier into boards.

After the puck carrier gets bumped a time or two by the two-man forechecking, he probably will decide his best way out is to pass the puck. You can plan on several of the passes being of the desperation type, and by placing your other players well, you can pick off these passes (see illustration).

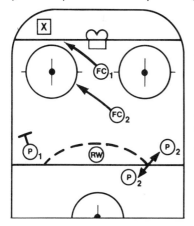

Forecheckers #**1** and #**2** try to: (1) Take puck away from the puck carrier and (2) force puck carrier to make a pass in hopes he will throw it up the wing where P_1 can intercept or up the center where **RW** can intercept.

It is important that P_1 (the puck-side pointman) stays inside the zone. He also should be prepared to move forward to check a wing breaking out and receiving a pass from the puck carrier.

RW must get into the "safety zone." He should pick up loose pucks thrown up the center, but should not move forward to attack a puck carrier. If the original puck carrier is able to beat the two forecheckers (by skating around them or by passing), the safety forward (**RW**) should swing back to cover his wing and leave the puck carrier to the pointmen, who also should be retreating to the defensive zone.

If the two forecheckers turn the puck carrier back and the puck switches to the other side, the forechecking **LW** should swing back to the safety zone and **RW** should move in to become forechecker #2. (See illustration below.) As the team becomes better at this system, you can have two forecheckers and one safetyman, but in the beginning you are better off to specify the offside wing as the safety; there is a much better chance of having one backchecker for sure this way.

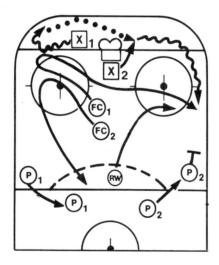

A forechecker can get the puck for your team by taking it away from the puck carrier or by forcing him to make a bad pass. Obviously, you will not be successful 100 percent of the time. Forecheckers should, however, force the puck carrier to move down the side of the rink rather than letting him come down the center and pick the side of your defensive zone he wishes to attack.

Backchecking—Middle Zone Coverage

It is most desirable that both offensive wings be covered. This means the puck carrier should be going one-on-one. This also does not happen very often, as was discussed in the Team Offense section.

Defensive Zone Coverage

Two basic patterns of coverage seem to be most popular:

1. Wing on Wing

The wings are responsible for their offensive wings from the time the forechecking pattern is broken until their team recovers the puck and goes on offense. The center covers the point on the puck side. The defenseman on the off puck-side stays near the front of the net, usually covering the offensive center. The defenseman on the puck side moves to help cover the puck carrier (usually a wing or the center), but does not "run out" to the point. The strength of this coverage is in having four men to cover three forwards. The weakness is that the center has a difficult time moving from point to point. It is usually a good defense for younger teams, because the offense cannot pass well enough to take advantage of the open pointman.

2. Wing on Point

Wings backcheck their offensive wings. At an appropriate time when his offensive wing does not have the puck and/or the defenseman on this side can assume responsibility for the offensive wing, the defensive wing leaves the offensive wing and moves to cover the point. The defensemen cover the zone in front of and to the side of the net. The center moves back in front of the net to work with the defensemen. The strength of this defense is that all five offensive players are covered one-on-one. The weaknesses are: (1) Often a mixup occurs as to when the defenseman becomes responsible for the wing and (2) the center, who most often is involved in deep forechecking, is late in getting back to help in front of the net.

Regardless of the coverage system, it is important for the defense to force the offensive players to the sides (away from the slot) and make them take poor shots on goal. The worst that happens to team defense is when a check is missed and players start "running" to try to help each other. Soon there are two, three or four defensive players bumping into each other, while the offense is building a two-on-one situation.

Man-Short Situations

The penalties assessed in hockey are more reasonable than in any other sport. The offender is penalized, but his team has an opportunity to prevent damage by working extra hard for two minutes (or five) to keep the other team from scoring.

Penalty situations cause you to change your forechecking and defensive coverage arrangements. Some suggest no forechecking when down one man. This seems a little generous. Rather, it is reasonable to offer at least token forechecking to apply enough pressure to force direction of play or a pass. There is always the possibility of a bad pass.

It is particularly important that both wings be backchecked. This forces the "power play" to use at least one pointman to gain a two-on-one entering the offensive zone.

Most teams use a type of zone coverage when playing four against five. This usually is referred to as the "box" — one defensive player on each corner of the box (illustration below left). The wing on the off puck-side should "collapse" the box somewhat to help out in the slot area (illustration below right).

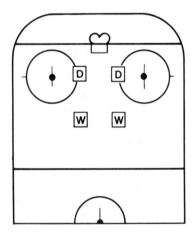 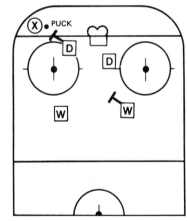

It is important for the defense to avoid "running" and to recognize that the objective is not to prevent *any* shots on goal, but to prevent the shot from the slot.

When your team is *down two men,* the usual approach is to put your fastest player out as a forward and have him chase the puck. In the defensive zone, the three defenders try to maintain a triangle — one point of the triangle on the puck and the others providing coverage in front of the net. (Illustrations below.) Be sure the three players you have on the ice are the quickest and most agile available at the time.

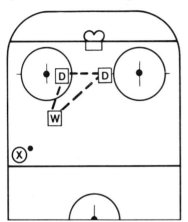
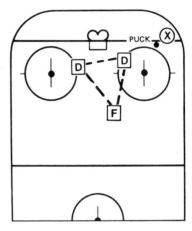

learning the fundamentals

The following drills have been selected to help you develop skill in each facet of hockey play. In addition to these drills, no doubt your coach will devise drills and exercises of his own to improve your team's overall play.

Skating Drills

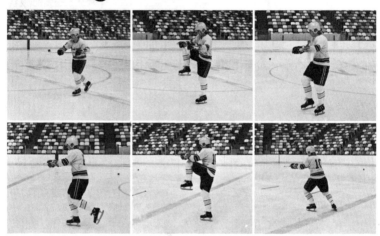

Knee Up Drill and Toes Up Drill

These drills are very similar and provide good balance exercise. Players should skate forward, bringing the knee or toes upward in four-stride intervals, alternating left and right legs.

Four-Stride Drill

This drill is used to help players develop a long, powerful stride. The player gains momentum by skating around the end perimeter of the rink (behind goals), then turns up ice near the corner face-off spot. From there the player is allowed four strides to skate the length of the ice.

Lateral Crossover Drill

Place several sticks on the ice, parallel to each other and about 12 inches apart. Players step quickly between each stick, then skate back to the end of the line to repeat the drill.

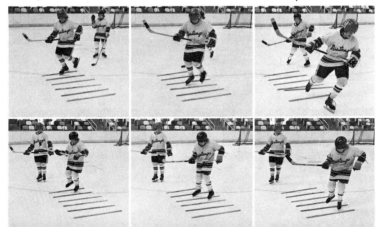

Swing Drill

While skating across the rink at the blue line or red line, the player "swings" out from the line on the inside edges of his skates. He then repeats the stride with the opposite foot. Players should feel strength and balance from skating on the inside edges.

This drill also may be performed by placing sticks on the ice ten feet apart and having players glide around the end of each stick on the outside leg.

Stickhandling Drills

Begin by practicing stickhandling moves while standing still, as nearly as possible in the basic position for skating forward. Remember the purpose of stickhandling: to fool the opposing player. Work on one move at a time. With a large number of players, work across the ice; with a smaller number, work down the ice and finish with shots on the net.

In all drills, players must learn to move the puck with a "soft" touch; stickhandling is a delicate art. After players learn the three basic stickhandling moves, they should try to put them together in combinations.

Block Drill

Position blocks about 10 to 15 feet apart, alternating one side and then the other. Players line up at the end and control the puck around each block.

Gate Drill

Sticks about three to four feet long are positioned on the ice some 12 to 18 inches apart. Player must move the puck from side to side and through the sticks.

Split Drill with Gates

Skate around sticks placed 12 to 18 inches apart and bring puck around to opposite side.

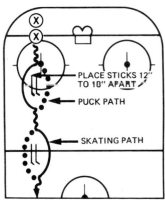

PLACE STICKS 12" TO 10" APART

PUCK PATH

SKATING PATH

One-Leg Drill

Stand on one leg while stickhandling from side to side, then jump to the other leg and repeat.

One-on-One Drill

This is the basic play in hockey. The player should try his moves against an opponent, attempting to fool him with stickhandling ability. The offensive player appears to have the advantage; for the most part he will "make" the play. The defensive player should be primarily concerned about playing the *body* of the offensive player, *not* the puck.

But *all* players are interested in getting the puck. Therefore, most defensive players can be enticed into playing the puck by the offensive player's use of good fakes and by his giving the impression that the puck can be taken away from him. If the defensive player cannot be faked and stays on the line between the offensive player and the goal, then passing as well as stickhandling is necessary to get around him or to gain better position with respect to the goal.

The ultimate objective is to get a good shot at the net, but more often good stickhandling will enable the offensive player to retain control of the puck until such time as he can pass to a teammate who is free for a shot. The ability to retain possession of the puck is most important to the offensive team and depends on good stickhandling. It should be noted that in one-on-one situations the defensive player "wins" about 70 percent of the time.

One-on-one is the best of all stickhandling drills because it is really what the game is all about — one person (or team) trying to score, the other trying to stop him (them).

Key to Diagrams
p. 92

Passing Drills

It is usually beneficial to begin passing drills with all players stationary. From there proceed by having the target moving and then onto having both passer and target moving.

Throwing the puck softly into a target zone ahead of a receiver is generally regarded as good passing technique. Coaches and players need to be especially patient in developing good passing techniques. Coordinating the speeds of the passer, the receiver and the puck — not to mention the positions of opposing players — is not easy.

Pass and Follow Drill

Player #**1** passes to #**2**. Player #**1** then skates to #**2**'s position.

Player #**2** passes to #**3**, then skates to #**3**'s position and so on until #**5** gets the puck, shoots, then goes to the end of the line so that the rotation can continue.

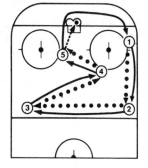

Automatic Passing

Place pucks in a circle as shown.

After coach starts the first three players, the drill continues without interruption.

Shooter passes puck to player #**1**; #**1** breaks up ice to red line and makes lateral pass to **A**; #**1** gets in line back of **B**; **A** takes pass, breaks on goal and shoots; then passes to #**10**. **A** goes to the back of the line.

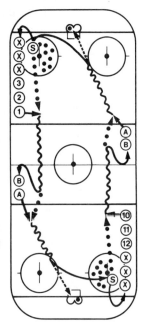

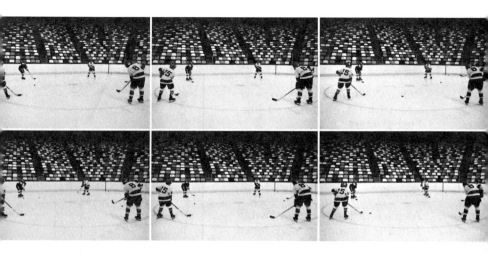

Circle Drills

Several drills can be performed from a basic circle position.

1. Each player has a puck which he passes to the player next to him. Pucks are received and passed continuously around the circle (see photo series above).
2. With one puck in the circle, the puck is passed from one player across the circle to another.
3. Puck is passed to a player across the circle, then passer skates across to the other side, replacing player to whom he passed (see photo series below).

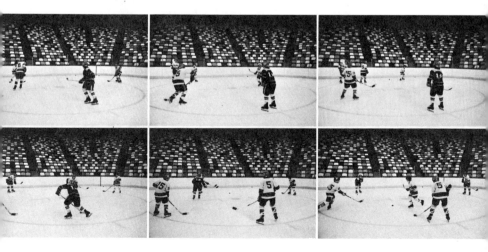

Three-on-Zero Drill

Players form three lines as shown.

"Ones" start three-on-zero; when Unit 1 crosses red line, "twos" start.

After shot on Goal A, each unit immediately picks up puck and heads back three-on-zero on Goal B.

As players improve, they switch lanes (crossing) as they move up and down the ice.

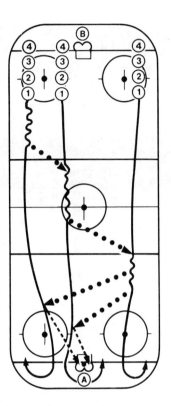

Flip Pass Drill

Place hockey stick flat upon the ice. Players alternate flipping pass over stick. First player to hit stick with puck "loses."

Shooting Drills

Forehand Shot Drill

Good drill for both shooters and the goalie. Shooters merely dribble in from either side or center of rink to make forehand shot on goal.

Backhand Shot Drill

Right-hand shooters line up on one side of the rink; left-hand shooters, on the other side. Shooters stickhandle around blocks placed on ice to make backhand shot on goal.

Tip-In Drill

Since many goals are scored on tip-ins, this is a good drill to condition you to look for the tip-in shot. X_1 passes to X_2 who in turn shoots while X_5 tips the shot in. Then X_3 passes to X_4 who shoots and again X_5 tips the shot on goal. After several repetitions players exchange positions.

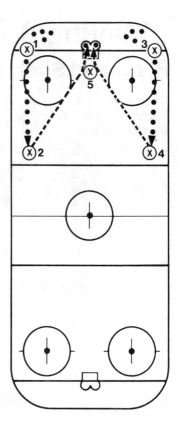

Shooting Alley Drill

Players merely stickhandle through prescribed course to make forehand or backhand shot on goal.

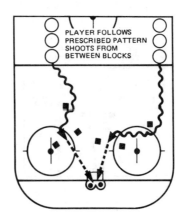

PLAYER FOLLOWS
PRESCRIBED PATTERN
SHOOTS FROM
BETWEEN BLOCKS

Two-Shot Drill

X_1 passes to **X**, who then skates in with puck two or three steps to shoot on goal. **X** follows shot while X_1 passes second puck in front of goal. **X** then makes second shot on goal.

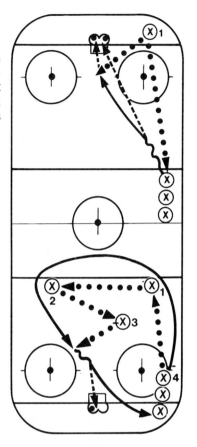

Checker Drill

X_4 passes to X_1. X_1 passes to X_2 who in turn passes to X_3. X_3 passes to X_4 who shoots on goal and moves to the end of the line.

Goalkeeping Drills

Daily drills for goaltenders should include (1) moving forward, backward and laterally, (2) stick-hand and catching-hand saves, (3) skate saves, (4) V drops, (5) stacking pads, (6) stick saves and poke checking and (7) skating.

Agility Exercises

Agility drills should be done "all out," with whistle signals: (1) dropping to the left knee and springing back up, (2) dropping to the right knee and springing back up, (3) dropping to both knees and springing back up, (4) dropping to stomach with stick extended and getting up.

Off-Season Work

Tennis, racquetball, table tennis, squash and other such sports are excellent off-season drills for goaltenders. Another drill is to place the net 20 feet in front of and facing a wall. The goalie stands in goal facing the wall, using stick and gloves only. The coach stands behind the net and throws rubber balls against the wall from various angles. The goaltender has little time to react to the balls as they rebound off the wall and toward the net.

Making the Pads a "Part" of the Goalie

There are several easy ways for the goalie to acquire the feel of the pads: Playing table tennis with the leg pads strapped on (this gives the player an opportunity to get used to the weight of the pads while moving from side to side) and wearing the pads at home, while studying, eating, reading and so on.

Deflecting shots to a predetermined area is also helpful. On any shot directly at him, the goalie should not kick at it or try to turn it into the corner. If the shot is directly at the pads, he should stop it with the pad and trap the puck on the pad with the catching hand. However, many shots are to one side or the other, and his pads are the only weapon the goalie has. To make this stop, the goalie must kick the puck with the leg pad, following through to direct it to the corner or sideboard. It is most important that the goalie watch the puck hit his pad.

The tap drill also helps give a goalie the feeling of his pads.

Defense against the Shot Drills
Multiple-Puck Drill

Ten pucks are lined up directly in front of the net, about 15 feet out. The goalie stands back in the net because he has to move faster in that position. The shooter then shoots the pucks, one after another in rapid succession.

Special Spot Drill

Six pucks are placed in a line, halfway between the special spot and the inner edge of the circle on both sides of the net. One shooter is placed in each circle. The shooter to the goalie's right shoots first; as soon as he has shot, the shooter on the left shoots and so on. The goalie should be given time to make the first save before the second shot is made. This drill aids a goalie's "recovery."

Semi-Circle Drill

Three or four players position themselves in a semi-circle in front of the net. They pass a puck between them rapidly, occasionally taking a shot at the net. This drill helps the goalie follow the puck while on his feet, and the occasional shot makes him more alert and develops quickness from a moving position.

Tap Drill

Coach or teammate uses handle end of hockey stick as target at which goalie kicks out with his foot. This is a good quick-reaction drill to condition the goalie in getting his foot out and up to make low-corner shot saves.

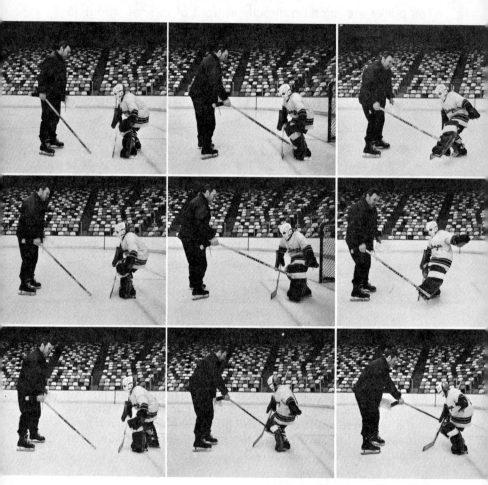

Scaling Puck Drill

With the goalie back in the net, the coach kneels about 15 feet in front of the net. Using 12 pucks, he scales (throws at ice level) them rapidly at the goalie. This drill quickens the skate save and helps develop the stick save.

Rope Demonstration

To explain the technique of playing the angles, the coach attaches two ropes, one on each side, to the goal posts. The coach holding the opposite ends of the rope in one hand represents the shooter. The area inside the rope represents the "angle." As the goalie moves out toward the shooter, the shooting angle is shown to decrease.

Turnaround Drill

This is a quick-reaction drill in which goalie begins by facing the back of the goal. Upon command, the goalie turns around to make a save on a puck thrown toward the goal.

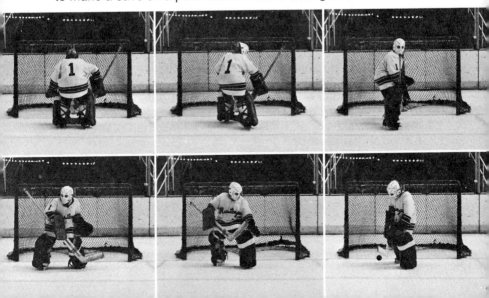

Who Should Play Where?

This is a big problem at all levels of youth hockey. For professional hockey, it is likely that a composite list of skills and traits could be developed for each position with a good degree of reliability. With young players, these skills are just forming; their physical attributes are changing gradually, and their motivation and desire can change almost overnight.

Here are some general guidelines and comments that may help in forming a team.

Goaltender

Most important player on the team. He must be a good skater (unfortunately, many times the player who is a poor skater ends up in goal; if this is the case, he must work very hard to improve his skating). He must have courage. Good hands are an asset; many goalies are catchers in baseball.

Defensemen

If there are several players who can score well, the best athlete should, perhaps, go on defense, even if he always has been a forward. The biggest problem for virtually all hockey teams is getting out of their own zone. The success of Bobby Orr certainly has made defense a more attractive position.

Defensemen must be agile and have good backward skating ability. They should be strong and courageous, able to take body contact and being hit by shots. They should be better-than-average stickhandlers and passers. (It is in this area that most of the difficulty occurs; too often the player who is the poor stickhandler and passer gets "put at defense.") It helps to have an even and cool disposition, for excitement often leads to mistakes, and mistakes by defensemen often equal a good shot on goal or a goal.

Care needs to be taken in "pairing" defensemen. Most important: One of each pair must have good ability to control the puck.

Forwards

Matching the forwards on a line can be important. Naturally, the best situation is when all forwards are able to do all things fairly well. Usually, however, they will have variations in abilities. Here are four important factors in considering a forward line: (1) speed, (2) goal scoring, (3) desire and ability to work on defensive play (backchecking) and (4) puck control and playmaking.

It is very important to understand that wide variations in skills and traits are evident in forwards, and the following guidelines may not apply all the time:

> WINGS — Strong, fast skaters. Good shots. Enough courage and strength to battle defensemen in front of the net and in the corners. Good passing skills.

> CENTER — Quick, agile skater. Good puck control, stickhandler and passer. Desire to "make the play" for his wings. Good "sense of the game." Good forechecker.

Note: As young players, it is a good idea to play as many positions as possible. Specializing at too young an age may cause limitations to your development in later years.

glossary of ice hockey terms

ATTACKING ZONE: Area between the blue line and the end boards in which the opponents' goal cage is located.

BACKCHECKING: Skating back toward own goal to help out the defense and to regain control of the puck.

BACK DIAGONAL PASS: Making a diagonal pass to a teammate behind you.

BLIND PASS: Passing the puck without looking.

BODYCHECK: Using the trunk of the body to check an opponent who has possession of the puck.

BREAKAWAY: Puck carrier skating toward his opponents' goal with only the goalkeeper to beat.

BREAKOUT PATTERN: The play employed to move the puck out of the defensive zone.

CENTER ZONE: The area between the blue lines.

CLEARING THE PUCK: The defending team getting the puck away from in front of its goal.

COVER UP: To guard an opponent in your defensive zone, thus preventing him from receiving a pass.

CUTTING: Crossover skating stride when turning.

DEFENSIVE ZONE: Area between the blue line and the end boards in which the team's own goal cage is located.

"DEKE": The movement a puck carrier uses to fake an opponent out of position.

DIGGING: Attempting to gain control of the puck in the corner from an opponent.

DRAW: Successfully getting puck back to a teammate on the face off.

DRIBBLE: Controlling the puck on the end of the stick.

DROP PASS: Stopping the puck dead and moving away, thus permitting a teammate who is coming from behind to pick it up.

FACE-OFF: Puck is dropped between two players to start or resume play.

FEEDING: Passing the puck to a teammate who is in a position to score a goal.

FINISHING: Scoring a goal.

FLIP: Lifting or flipping the puck over an opponent's stick to a teammate.

FORECHECKING: Harassing opponents in their defensive zone when they have gained control of the puck. Breaks up the play before it gets started.

FREEZING THE PUCK: Holding the puck against the boards or goal with the skate or stick.

HAT TRICK: A player scores three goals in one game.

HEADMANNING: Passing the puck ahead to a teammate.

HIP CHECK: Using the hip to knock an opponent in possession of the puck offstride.

ON-THE-FLY: Changing or substituting players while play is in progress.

"POINTS": The position of defensemen just inside their opponents' blue line when their team is on the attack.

POKE CHECK: Making a sudden jab at the puck with the stick extended far out in front.

POWER PLAY: The play of a team with a manpower advantage because of a penalty to its opponents.

PULLING THE GOALIE: Substituting a player — most often a forward — for the goalkeeper, usually done in the closing minutes or seconds of the game by a team that is behind in goals to add more offensive power.

REBOUND: Puck that bounces off goalie or goal post.

SAVE: The goalkeeper preventing the puck from entering goal.

SHORT HANDED: A team playing with fewer players than the opponents because of a penalty.

SLOW WHISTLE: When the puck is in the possession of a team at the time the opposing team commits a foul, the referee postpones calling the violation until the offending team secures possession and control of the puck.

STICK LIE: Angle between the blade and the handle of the stick constitutes the "lie."

STOPS AND STARTS: A skating drill.

SWEEP CHECK: With a sweeping motion and with the entire stick flat on the ice, the player attempts to get the puck away from an opponent.

TELEGRAPHING: Looking directly at a teammate before passing him the puck, thus indicating to the opponent the direction in which the pass will be made.

TRAILER: A player following a teammate who is in possession of the puck.

UNCOVERED: Attacking player left unguarded in front of the net.